WILLIAMS-SONOMA

Asian Flavors

GENERAL EDITOR

Chuck Williams

RECIPES

Joyce Jue

PHOTOGRAPHY

Richard Eskite

TIME
LIFE
BOOKS

TIME-LIFE BOOKS
Time-Life Books is a division of Time Life Inc.
Time-Life is a trademark of Time Warner Inc. U.S.A.

TIME-LIFE CUSTOM PUBLISHING
Vice President and Publisher: Terry Newell
Vice President of Sales and Marketing: Neil Levin
Director of Financial Operations: J. Brian Birky
Director of Acquisitions: Jennifer L. Pearce

WILLIAMS-SONOMA
Founder and Vice-Chairman: Chuck Williams
Associate Book Buyer: Cecilia Michaelis

WELDON OWEN INC.
President: John Owen
Vice President and Publisher: Wendely Harvey
Chief Operating Officer: Larry Partington
Vice President International Sales: Stuart Laurence
Managing Editor: Val Cipollone
Consulting Editor: Norman Kolpas
Copy Editor: Judith Dunham
Design: Kari Perin, Perin+Perin
Production Director: Stephanie Sherman
Production Manager: Christine DePedro
Production Editor: Kathryn Meehan
Food Stylist: Pouké
Prop Stylist: Sara Slavin
Photo Production Coordinator: Juliann Harvey
Photo Assistant: Kevin Hossler
Food Styling Assistant: Jeff Tucker
Glossary Illustrations: Alice Harth

A NOTE ON WEIGHTS AND MEASURES
All recipes include customary U.S. and metric
measurements. Metric conversions are based on a
standard developed for these books and have been
rounded off. Actual weights may vary.

The Williams-Sonoma Lifestyle Series
conceived and produced by Weldon Owen Inc.
814 Montgomery Street, San Francisco, CA 94133

In collaboration with Williams-Sonoma
3250 Van Ness Avenue, San Francisco, CA 94109

Separations by Colourscan Overseas Co. Pte. Ltd.
Printed in Singapore by Tien Wah Press (Pte.) Ltd.

A WELDON OWEN PRODUCTION
Copyright © 1999 Weldon Owen Inc.
All rights reserved, including the right of reproduc-
tion in whole or in part in any form.

First printed in 1999
10 9 8 7 6 5 4 3 2 1

Library of Congress
Cataloging-in-Publication Data

Jue, Joyce
    Asian Flavors / general editor, Chuck Williams;
recipes by Joyce Jue; photography by Richard Eskite.
        p. cm. — (Williams-Sonoma lifestyles)
    Includes index.
    ISBN 0-7370-2023-7
    1. Cookery, Asian I. Williams, Chuck
II. Title III. Series.
TX724.5.A1j82   1999
641.595— dc21   99-10020
                                            CIP

A NOTE ON NUTRITIONAL ANALYSIS
Each recipe is analyzed for significant nutrients per
serving. Not included in the analysis are ingredients
that are optional or added to taste, or are suggested
as an alternative or substitution either in the recipe
or in the recipe introduction or accompanying tip. In
recipes that yield a range of servings, the analysis is
for the middle of that range.

Contents

Welcome

Not so long ago, "Asian food" meant Chinese food, more specifically the Cantonese-style cooking many Westerners grew up enjoying when they went out to eat. Today, Westerners are familiar with many different kinds of Asian food, from Chinese regional cuisines to the cuisines of Japan, Thailand, Vietnam, Korea, India, and Indonesia. This growing popularity of Asian cuisines has had a significant influence on Western cooks in restaurants and home kitchens alike.

The welcoming of Asian flavors into the mainstream is the inspiration behind this book. Its 50 kitchen-tested recipes highlight the kinds of widely varied, authentic regional dishes that have become popular in the West. The introductory text and comprehensive glossary provide all the information you need to identify and obtain Asian ingredients, demystify Asian cooking techniques, and incorporate them into your approach to cooking.

I encourage you to begin your own exploration of Asian flavors, using this book as your guide. An exciting, and delicious, journey awaits.

East Meets West

Eastern influences are right at home in Western settings. Here, fresh fruit (above) is used as an attractive still life. Sizzling Rice Cake Soup with Crab (right) can be a starter or light main course.

Planning an Asian Meal

The recipes in this book are organized into categories familiar to Western cooks. This approach aims to help you integrate the dishes into Western-style menus, whether you serve just one dish or compose an entire menu. Knowing how these dishes are authentically presented may inspire you to find new ways to enjoy them.

What Westerners consider appetizers—such as Chicken Satay with Peanut Sauce (page 31)—most people in Asian countries eat as snacks or light meals throughout the day. Soups are integral to traditional meals.

Light broth-based soups such as Miso Soup with Tofu and Mushrooms (page 27) or Sour Seafood Soup (page 20) are sipped from course to course and may play the role of beverage.

Salads and noodle dishes are often served as light one-dish meals, which makes sense considering the satisfaction to be found in such recipes as Pad Thai (page 57) and Rice Stick Noodles with Grilled Pork (page 61). Side dishes like Dry-Fried Green Beans (page 62) and Stir-Fried Pea Shoots with Garlic (page 66) occupy supporting positions, just as vegetables do in Western meals.

Similarly, main courses like Miso-Glazed Sea Bass (page 97) or Dry Beef Curry (page 94) take center stage at full-scale family meals. Asian desserts are usually light fruit dishes, perfectly attuned to today's interest in healthful eating. Orange Slices in Rose Flower Water (page 104) is a good example.

Preparing Asian Food

A quick glance at the recipes in this book reveals that many possess two notable characteristics.

First, although the foods are prepared using familiar cooking methods, the ingredients may be unfamiliar to Westerners. The photographs on pages 10–11 and the glossary on pages 108–111 aim to give you the knowledge and confidence to seek out these items in Asian markets and well-stocked food stores.

The other key feature is the extensive instructions given in most recipes for preparing individual ingredients. Being preparation-intensive, these recipes may at first seem complicated. Bear in mind, however, that advance preparation streamlines the final cooking process, which often moves along quite quickly. Stir-frying is a prime example of fast-paced cooking.

Using Asian Equipment

Several pieces of Asian cooking equipment, such as a mortar and pestle, a wok, a bamboo sushi mat, and a bamboo steamer basket, will also help streamline food preparation. These items may be found in Asian markets or well-stocked kitchenware stores. You can easily make do, however, with Western-style equivalents—substituting, respectively, an electric spice grinder, a large frying pan, a sheet of heavy-duty plastic wrap, and a metal steamer for the equipment mentioned above.

Asian-inspired serving pieces, though not required, can add to the aesthetic pleasure of a meal. Browse local Asian markets as well as kitchen supply and housewares shops and see what you can find.

A collection of Asian equipment (below, left) and serving pieces (below, right) is a welcome addition to the Western kitchen.

Rice Ribbon Noodles

Galangal

Kaffir Lime Leaves

Sauces and Seasonings

Daikon

Bean Thread Vermicelli

Sugarcane

Shanghai-Style Noodles

Pea Shoots

Asparagus Beans

Chinese-Style Egg Noodles

Green Papaya

Rice Stick Noodles

Buckwheat Noodles

Basic Techniques

The recipes in this book call for and explain preparation and cooking techniques common to many Asian kitchens. These techniques, while unfamiliar to some Western cooks, are easy to master, as demonstrated by the three step-by-step sequences shown here.

ROLLING SUSHI

1. With moistened hands, spread rice on a lightly toasted nori sheet aligned on a bamboo sushi mat. Arrange the filling in an even horizontal strip across the rice. Lift the nearest edge of mat, nori, and rice over the filling to seal it inside.

2. Continue to lift and press on the mat to form a snug roll. Pull back on the mat as you push and roll the nori and rice away from you.

Stir-frying, as demonstrated on the opposite page, proceeds quickly and efficiently when all the ingredients are prepared and assembled near the stove top before cooking starts.

STIR-FRYING

1. Heat a wok over medium-high heat. Pour in oil and, when it is hot, add aromatic ingredients. Stir and toss with a long-handled spatula.

2. Raise the heat. Add the remaining ingredients, as the recipe directs, and stir and toss vigorously until cooked.

MAKING A SPICE PASTE

1. Assemble the spices. Put an ingredient in a mortar and begin pounding with a pestle. Add and pound the remaining ingredients one after the other.

2. Continue pounding and grinding the spices against the mortar to blend them into a smooth paste. Add liquid—here, soy sauce—and pound to incorporate.

STEAMED RICE

Though the rice is boiled, it is called steamed rice.

2 cups (14 oz/440 g) long-grain white rice
2¼ cups (18 fl oz/560 ml) water

❀ *Rinse the rice with cold water until the rinse water runs clear. Drain well and place in a 2–2½-qt (2–2.5-l) saucepan. Add the water.*

❀ *Place over high heat and bring to a boil. Stir briefly and continue boiling until the water on the surface is completely absorbed and small pits have formed. Cover, reduce the heat to very low, and cook, undisturbed, for 20 minutes.*

❀ *Remove from the heat and let stand, covered, for at least 10 minutes or for up to 40 minutes before serving.*

❀ *Wet a wooden spoon and use it to fluff the rice. Serve hot.*

MAKES 4–5 CUPS
(20–25 OZ/625–780 G)

Beverages

It is fun to use a special Vietnamese drip coffeemaker to make iced coffee (top). You'll achieve similar results brewing the coffee with a Melita®-style filter. Thai Limeade (bottom) is sweet-tart and refreshing.

Vietnamese Iced Coffee

This drink, for those who like their coffee sweet and strong, is served during and after meals.

1 cup (8 fl oz/250 ml) water
3 tablespoons sweetened condensed milk, more if needed
3 tablespoons dark-roast medium-grind French coffee
ice cubes

❀ In a teakettle or saucepan, bring the water to a boil. Pour the condensed milk into an 8–fl oz (250-ml) glass that is about 3½ inches (9 cm) wide at the top. Spoon the ground coffee into the filter and screw the top filter on tight. Set the filter on top of the glass.

❀ Spoon 2 tablespoons boiling water into the filter to moisten the ground coffee. Allow the coffee to absorb the water, about 30 seconds. Bring the coffee filter and glass and the remaining boiling water to the table. Slowly pour the water into the filter and allow the coffee to slowly drip until all the water is used, about 10 minutes. Add ice cubes and more milk, if desired. Serve cold.

SERVES 1

Thai Limeade

Fresh limeade is a cool and soothing complement to the hot, spicy flavors of Thai food. Thais use lime rinds to flavor the drink, which is sweet or salty. This is a sweet version with just a touch of salt.

10 large limes
3½ cups (28 fl oz/875 ml) water
¾ cup (6 oz/185 g) sugar
1 teaspoon salt
4 ice cubes, plus more as needed

❀ Thoroughly wash the limes under cold running water. Juice the limes; you should have about 1½ cups (12 fl oz/375 ml) juice. Place the juice in a bowl or pitcher and the rinds in a large heatproof glass bowl.

❀ In a saucepan, bring the water, sugar, and salt to a boil. Pour over the rinds and let stand for 15 minutes. Strain and add to the lime juice; discard the rinds. Add the 4 ice cubes to cool the mixture. Cover and refrigerate for at least 1 hour or up to 2 days. Pour into ice-filled, tall glasses and serve.

SERVES 8

Peach Lassi with Rose Flower Water

Lassi, a blended yogurt drink, is one of the most popular chilled beverages in India. Sweet or salty, it is blended with crushed ice or flavored with fresh fruit. Yogurt-based drinks cool the heat of spicy foods.

1 teaspoon fennel seeds
3 cups (24 oz/750 g) low-fat plain
   yogurt
2 peaches, peeled and chopped
½ cup (4 oz/125 g) sugar
¼ cup (½ oz/15 g) well-packed fresh
   mint leaves, plus mint sprigs for
   garnish
¼ cup (2 fl oz/60 ml) ice water
1 tablespoon lime juice
1½ teaspoons rose flower water
10 ice cubes

❀ In a small frying pan over low heat, toast the fennel seeds, stirring occasionally, until fragrant, 3–5 minutes. Transfer to a spice grinder and grind to a powder, or transfer to a mortar and grind with a pestle.

❀ Place the yogurt, ground fennel, peaches, sugar, mint leaves, ice water, lime juice, rose flower water, and ice cubes in a blender. Process until frothy, about 2 minutes. Pour into chilled tall glasses and garnish with mint sprigs. Serve immediately.

SERVES 6

Iced Litchi Tea

Litchi tea was quite fashionable in the 1950s and is making a comeback as an iced drink. Fresh litchis are available only in midsummer, but canned litchis are sold year-round. Chinese litchi black tea can be found in Asian markets.

8 cups (64 fl oz/2 l) water
2 tablespoons Chinese litchi black
   tea leaves
ice cubes
18 fresh litchis, peeled, or
   18 canned litchis, drained
sugar to taste

❀ In a teakettle or saucepan, bring the water to a boil. Pour 2 cups (16 fl oz/500 ml) of the boiling water into a large teapot or heatproof pitcher. Pour out the water. Place the tea leaves into the teapot or pitcher and add the remaining 6 cups (48 fl oz/1.5 l) boiling water. Cover and steep for 15 minutes. Let cool. Strain into another pitcher and discard the leaves.

❀ Half-fill 6 tall glasses with ice cubes and pour in the tea. Place 3 litchis in each glass; they will eventually sink to the bottom. Offer the sugar to add to taste. Eat the litchis as a treat with the tea.

SERVES 6

Planning Menus

Traditional Asian menus are composed of many dishes served all at once. In Western menus, one dish usually takes center stage. Asian dishes are perfectly suited to this custom. In planning a menu, begin with the recipe that you find most exciting, then choose other recipes that will complement its flavor, texture, and overall feel—whether delicate or homespun. The menus offered here follow this approach. They have been organized, for the most part, by country of origin. By all means, feel free to mix and match recipes as you plan your meal.

Japanese Inspired

Miso Soup with Tofu
and Mushrooms
PAGE 27

California Rolls
PAGE 40

Green Tea Ice Cream

Casual Vietnamese

Spring Rolls with Salmon
and Mango
PAGE 19

Kettle-Seared
Garlic-Pepper Mussels
PAGE 85

Lemon Sorbet

Fiery Thai

Spicy Stuffed Omelet Pouches
PAGE 36

Striped Bass Grilled
in Banana Leaves
PAGE 69

Orange Slices
in Rose Flower Water
PAGE 104

Indian Inspired

Tandoori Chicken and
Toasted Pappadams
PAGE 73

Steamed Basmati Rice

Curried Potatoes,
Cauliflower, and Peas
PAGE 74

Small Bites

Crispy Vegetable Crêpes
PAGE 24

Crab Cakes with Sweet-and-
Sour Cucumber Salad
PAGE 28

Chicken Satay
with Peanut Sauce
PAGE 31

Light Chinese

Sizzling Rice Cake Soup
with Crab
PAGE 35

Dry-Fried Green Beans
PAGE 62

Fortune Cookies

Thai Dinner

Scallops, Eggplant, and Squash
in Green Curry Sauce
PAGE 77

Spicy Asparagus Bean Salad
PAGE 43

Black Sticky Rice
with Coconut Cream
PAGE 103

A Bowl of Noodles

Rice Stick Noodles
with Grilled Pork
PAGE 61

Mango and Pineapple Sorbet
PAGE 99

Vietnamese Iced Coffee
PAGE 14

Easy Stir-Fry

Chicken and Asparagus with
Spicy Black Bean Sauce
PAGE 70

Steamed Rice
PAGE 13

Stir-Fried Pea Shoots
with Garlic
PAGE 66

Curry and Spice

Dry Beef Curry
PAGE 94

Steamed Basmati Rice

Tangy Mango Relish
PAGE 58

Peach Lassi
with Rose Flower Water
PAGE 15

Spring Rolls with Salmon and Mango

PREP TIME: 1¼ HOURS, PLUS
1 HOUR FOR CHILLING

COOKING TIME: 15 MINUTES

INGREDIENTS

4 oz (125 g) dried thin rice
    vermicelli noodles

1 lb (500 g) salmon fillets

1 large carrot, peeled and very finely
    julienned

1 teaspoon sugar

16 dried rice paper rounds, each
    8½ inches (21.5 cm) in diameter

16 large red-leaf lettuce leaves, ribs
    removed

1 mango, peeled and cut into slices
    3–4 inches (7.5–10 cm) long and
    ¼ inch (6 mm) thick

1 avocado, pitted, peeled, and cut
    into slices 3–4 inches (7.5–10 cm)
    long and ¼ inch (6 mm) thick

16 fresh mint leaves, shredded

32 sprigs of fresh cilantro (fresh
    coriander)

Garlic-Lime Dipping Sauce *(page 61)*

PREP TIP: To speed the assembling
of the rolls, have ready several damp-
ened clean kitchen towels. As you
dip the rice paper rounds into the
water, lay them on a damp towel,
then cover with another damp towel.
Continue making layers of towels
and rice paper until you have used
the 16 rounds.

SERVES 8

❊ Place the noodles in a bowl and add water to cover. Let stand until
soft and pliable, about 15 minutes. Bring a large pot two-thirds full of
water to a boil. Drain the noodles, add to the boiling water, remove from
the heat, and let stand for 2 minutes. Drain and rinse with cold water.
Drain thoroughly and set aside.

❊ Pour water to a depth of 3 inches (7.5 cm) in a wide, deep frying pan
just large enough to hold the salmon in a single layer. Place over high
heat and bring to just below a boil so that the water shimmers with
movement but does not bubble. Slip the salmon into the water and
poach, uncovered, until the flesh easily flakes with a fork, 5–10 minutes.
Using a spatula, transfer the salmon to a plate and refrigerate for 1 hour.
Cut into 16 thin slices about 4 inches (10 cm) long.

❊ In a small bowl, combine the carrot and sugar. Let stand until the
carrot is softened, about 10 minutes.

❊ Fill a pie dish with warm water. Dampen 2 kitchen towels and lay on
a work surface. Dip 1 rice paper round at a time into the water and lay flat
on the towels. Continue dipping the rounds and arranging in a single layer
without overlapping on the towels. Allow to soften 1–2 minutes.

❊ When the rounds resemble wet wrinkled tissue, place 1 lettuce leaf
across the lower third of each round, leaving a 1-inch (2.5-cm) border
on the right and left edges. Spread a small amount (about one-sixteenth)
of the noodles over the lettuce in a line about 5 inches (13 cm) long by
1½ inches (4 cm) wide. Arrange one-sixteenth of the carrots, a few mango
slices, a salmon slice, a few avocado slices, and a few shreds of mint
over the noodles. Fold up the bottom edge of the rice paper round and
roll once over the ingredients, tucking them into a tight roll 5 inches (13 cm)
long. Fold in the right and left edges to enclose the filling. Place 2 sprigs
of cilantro over the roll and finish rolling. Set, seam side down, on a
baking sheet, cover with a damp kitchen towel, and set in a cool spot
while making the remaining rolls.

❊ Leave the rolls whole or cut each into 3 or 4 pieces. Serve at room
temperature with the dipping sauce.

NUTRITIONAL ANALYSIS PER SERVING: Calories 341 (Kilojoules 1,432); Protein 14 g;
Carbohydrates 49 g; Total Fat 10 g; Saturated Fat 2 g; Cholesterol 33 mg; Sodium 71 mg;
Dietary Fiber 2 g

Sour Seafood Soup

PREP TIME: 1 HOUR

COOKING TIME: 25 MINUTES

INGREDIENTS

2 tablespoons vegetable oil

½ lb (250 g) large shrimp (prawns), peeled and deveined, shells reserved

8 green serrano chiles, halved

6 slices fresh galangal or 3 pieces dried galangal

4 stalks lemongrass, cut into 2-inch (5-cm) pieces and crushed

6 cups (48 fl oz/1.5 l) chicken broth

8 fresh, frozen, or dried kaffir lime leaves

1 cup (4 oz/125 g) drained, canned whole straw mushrooms

1 cup (4 oz/125 g) drained, canned baby corn, cut into 1½-inch (4-cm) lengths

1 tablespoon Thai roasted chile paste

½ lb (250 g) mussels, scrubbed and debearded just before cooking

½ lb (250 g) bay scallops

¼ lb (125 g) cleaned squid, cut into rings ½ inch (12 mm) wide

3 tablespoons Thai fish sauce

2 tablespoons lime juice, or more to taste

1 red serrano chile, sliced crosswise, for garnish

2 tablespoons coarsely chopped fresh cilantro (fresh coriander), for garnish

Lemongrass, galangal (also known as Siamese ginger), and kaffir lime leaves are the three essential ingredients that characterize this classic Thai soup. Be sure to use Thai roasted chile paste (*nam prik pao* in Thai) and Thai fish sauce rather than the Chinese equivalents.

SERVES 6

❀ In a saucepan over medium-high heat, warm the oil. Add the shrimp shells and sauté until bright orange, about 1 minute. Add the green serrano chiles, galangal, lemongrass, chicken broth, and lime leaves and bring to a boil. Reduce the heat to low and simmer, uncovered, for 15 minutes.

❀ Strain the stock through a colander placed over a stockpot; discard the shells and seasoning ingredients. Add the mushrooms, corn, and chile paste and stir to combine. Bring to a boil over high heat, uncovered. Add the shrimp and mussels, discarding any mussels that do not close to the touch. Cook, uncovered, until the shrimp turn bright orange and the mussels begin to open, about 3 minutes. Stir in the scallops and squid, and cook, uncovered, until the scallops and squid begin to feel firm, about 1 minute longer. Stir in the fish sauce and lime juice. Taste and adjust the seasonings. Discard any mussels that did not open.

❀ Ladle the soup into warmed bowls, garnish with the red serrano chile and cilantro, and serve at once.

NUTRITIONAL ANALYSIS PER SERVING: Calories 199 (Kilojoules 836); Protein 21 g; Carbohydrates 8 g; Total Fat 9 g; Saturated Fat 2 g; Cholesterol 107 mg; Sodium 1,586 mg; Dietary Fiber 1 g

Savory Vegetable Fritters

PREP TIME: 45 MINUTES

COOKING TIME: 20 MINUTES

INGREDIENTS

1½ cups (6 oz/185 g) sifted chick-
  pea (garbanzo bean) flour, or
  more as needed

1½ teaspoons salt

1 teaspoon garam masala

1 teaspoon ground coriander

1 teaspoon baking powder

¼ teaspoon turmeric

1 green chile, seeded and finely
  chopped, or ¼ teaspoon cayenne
  pepper

1 tablespoon lemon juice

⅔ cup (5 fl oz/160 ml) water, or
  more as needed

1 small yam, about 3 oz (90 g),
  peeled and cut into ⅜-inch
  (1-cm) dice

1 cup (2 oz/60 g) small broccoli florets

1 small Asian (slender) eggplant
  (aubergine), cut into ⅜-inch
  (1-cm) dice

6 spinach leaves, coarsely chopped

½ red bell pepper (capsicum), cut
  into ⅜-inch (1-cm) dice

peanut or corn oil for frying

PREP TIP: The amount of batter
this recipe makes is just enough to
bind 3½ cups (17½ oz/545 g) diced
vegetables. Save any excess diced
vegetables for a soup or stir-fry.

One bite will confirm why these deep-fried fritters, called *pakora*, are one of India's most popular afternoon snacks. If the prepared spice blend called garam masala is not available, try mixing your own blend of the four "C" spices: ¼ teaspoon each ground cumin, ground coriander, ground cloves, and ground cinnamon. The fritters can be served on their own. They are also delicious with a fruit chutney such as tamarind or ginger chutney.

SERVES 6–8

❋ To make the batter, in a bowl, combine the 1½ cups (6 oz/185 g) flour, salt, garam masala, coriander, baking powder, turmeric, and chile or cayenne. Add the lemon juice and slowly mix in ⅓ cup (3 fl oz/80 ml) of the water, stirring to remove any lumps. Add only enough additional water, 1 tablespoon at a time, until the mixture is the consistency of a thick cake batter. Cover and let stand for 10 minutes.

❋ In a large bowl, toss together the yam, broccoli, eggplant, spinach, and bell pepper. You should have 3½ cups (17½ oz/545 g) vegetables; do not use more than this amount. Again, adjust the batter by adding flour or water, until it is the consistency of a thick cake batter. Add the vegetables to the batter and stir thoroughly to combine. The vegetables should hold together when scooped up with a tablespoon.

❋ In a large, deep frying pan over medium-high heat, pour oil to a depth of 2 inches (5 cm) and heat until 360°F (182°C) on a deep-frying thermometer. Working in batches, carefully drop the mixture, 1 tablespoon at a time, into the oil, without crowding. Fry until golden brown, about 3 minutes. Using a slotted spoon, transfer the fritters to paper towels to drain.

❋ Serve hot or at room temperature.

NUTRITIONAL ANALYSIS PER SERVING: Calories 214 (Kilojoules 899); Protein 5 g; Carbohydrates 20 g; Total Fat 13 g; Saturated Fat 2 g; Cholesterol 0 mg; Sodium 582 mg; Dietary Fiber 3 g

Crispy Vegetable Crêpes

PREP TIME: 1 HOUR

COOKING TIME: 10 MINUTES

INGREDIENTS

1¼ cups (6½ oz/200 g) rice flour

1 teaspoon turmeric

½ teaspoon salt, plus salt to taste

½ teaspoon sugar

1 cup (8 fl oz/250 ml) unsweetened
coconut milk

2 green (spring) onions, thinly sliced

½ lb (250 g) skinless, boneless chicken
breast halves

½ lb (250 g) medium shrimp (prawns)

6 cloves garlic, minced

6 shallots, thinly sliced

3 cups (15 oz/470 g) peeled and
finely shredded carrots

1 red bell pepper (capsicum), seeded
and finely julienned

2 yellow summer squashes, julienned

1½–2 lb (750 g–1 kg) mung bean
sprouts

2 cups (4 oz/125 g) small broccoli
florets

½ cup (½ oz/15 g) each fresh cilantro
(fresh coriander) leaves and fresh
mint leaves

¼ cup (¼ oz/7 g) loosely packed
fresh Thai or sweet basil leaves

6 tablespoons (3 fl oz/90 ml) peanut
or vegetable oil

ground pepper to taste

Garlic-Lime Dipping Sauce *(page 61)*

Expect the unexpected with your first bite of these crisp, golden Vietnamese crêpes filled with crunchy vegetables and both chicken and shrimp. You can use two woks or frying pans to cook two crêpes at once for your waiting guests.

SERVES 6

❀ In a bowl, combine the rice flour, turmeric, ½ teaspoon salt, and sugar. Add the coconut milk, green onions, and 1 cup (8 fl oz/250 ml) water, and blend thoroughly. Cover and refrigerate until ready to cook.

❀ Cut the chicken crosswise into thin strips. Shell and devein the shrimp, then halve lengthwise and pat dry. Divide the chicken, shrimp, garlic, shallots, carrots, bell pepper, squashes, bean sprouts, broccoli, cilantro, mint, and basil into 6 portions each.

❀ Heat a nonstick wok or nonstick 9-inch (23-cm) frying pan over medium-high heat. Add 1 tablespoon of the oil, one-sixth of the garlic, and one-sixth of the shallots and toss and stir until golden brown, about 1 minute. Add one-sixth each of the chicken and shrimp and toss and stir until the chicken is opaque, about 2 minutes. Season with salt and pepper. Evenly spread the chicken mixture on the pan bottom.

❀ Stir the batter until smooth. If it is too thick, add enough water, 1 tablespoon at a time, until it is the consistency of heavy cream. Pour ⅓ cup (3 fl oz/80 ml) into the pan and tilt the pan to spread the batter evenly over the pan bottom and up the sides. Scatter one-sixth each of the carrots, bell pepper, squashes, bean sprouts, and broccoli in the center. Cover, reduce the heat to medium, and cook until steam seeps out from under the lid, about 4 minutes. Uncover, raise the heat to medium-high, and cook until the crêpe shrinks away from the pan sides, about 2 minutes longer. Scatter one-sixth each of the cilantro, mint, and basil over the vegetables. Using a spatula, lift the edge to check if the underside is crisp and brown, then fold the crêpe like an omelet and slide onto a plate.

❀ Cut the crêpe crosswise into 4–6 pieces and serve immediately with the dipping sauce. Prepare the remaining crêpes.

NUTRITIONAL ANALYSIS PER SERVING: Calories 487 (Kilojoules 2,045); Protein 24 g; Carbohydrates 49 g; Total Fat 24 g; Saturated Fat 10 g; Cholesterol 69 mg; Sodium 314 mg; Dietary Fiber 6 g

Miso Soup with Tofu and Mushrooms

PREP TIME: 15 MINUTES

COOKING TIME: 15 MINUTES

INGREDIENTS

1 piece kombu seaweed, about
   4 inches (10 cm) long

4 cups (32 fl oz/1 l) water

1 cup (½ oz/15 g) loosely packed
   dried bonito flakes

⅓ cup (3½ oz/105 g) red or white
   miso

1 tablespoon mirin or sake

2 oz (60 g) fresh enoki mushrooms
   and/or fresh shiitake mushrooms

¼ lb (125 g) soft tofu, cut into ½-inch
   (12-mm) cubes

1 green (spring) onion, including
   tender green tops, cut on the
   diagonal into thin slices

PREP TIP: If you can't find fresh
enoki or fresh shiitake mushrooms,
feel free to use ordinary white mushrooms instead.

Miso soup is enjoyed in Japan throughout the day. It is served for breakfast because it is quick to prepare. At dinnertime, this light soup begins or ends the meal. Miso is a nutritious protein-rich paste made from fermented ground soybeans mixed with rice, wheat, or barley. Red *(aka)* miso or white *(shiro)* miso can be used to make this soup; the former has a heartier flavor. Kombu seaweed, a form of sea kelp, is sold as dried strips in Asian markets and health-food stores. Keep the soup from boiling, which destroys its delicate flavors.

SERVES 4–6

✲ Using a damp kitchen towel, wipe, but do not wash, the kombu. In a saucepan over medium heat, combine the kombu and the water. Slowly bring almost to a boil, then remove the kombu. Return the water to a boil and add the bonito flakes; do not stir. Immediately remove from the heat and let the flakes sink to the bottom of the pan. Pour the stock through a very fine-mesh sieve set over a large bowl. Discard the flakes.

✲ Return ½ cup (4 fl oz/125 ml) of the stock to the saucepan, add the miso and stir until thoroughly combined. Add the remaining stock and the mirin or sake. If using enoki mushrooms, cut off the lower portion of the stems and discard. If using shiitakes, cut off the stems and discard. Thinly slice the caps. Bring the stock almost to a boil over medium heat. Add the mushrooms and tofu. Remove from the heat.

✲ Ladle the soup into warmed bowls, garnish with the green onion, and serve at once.

NUTRITIONAL ANALYSIS PER SERVING: Calories 70 (Kilojoules 294); Protein 5 g; Carbohydrates 8 g; Total Fat 2 g; Saturated Fat 0 g; Cholesterol 2 mg; Sodium 832 mg; Dietary Fiber 1 g

Crab Cakes with Sweet-and-Sour Cucumber Salad

PREP TIME: 45 MINUTES, PLUS
30 MINUTES FOR CHILLING

COOKING TIME: 15 MINUTES

INGREDIENTS

½ lb (250 g) ground (minced) pork
butt

2 shallots, finely minced, plus I large
shallot, finely sliced

I red serrano chile, minced

I green (spring) onion, finely sliced

¼ cup (I oz/30 g) finely diced red
bell pepper (capsicum)

3 tablespoons coarsely chopped
fresh cilantro (fresh coriander)

2 tablespoons panko or fine dried
white bread crumbs, or as needed,
plus I cup (4 oz/125 g) for coating

I tablespoon fish sauce

I teaspoon ground pepper

I teaspoon salt

¼ teaspoon plus 2 tablespoons sugar

I egg, lightly beaten

½ lb (250 g) cooked fresh crabmeat,
flaked

½ cup (4 fl oz/125 ml) rice vinegar

½ English (hothouse) cucumber,
peeled, quartered lengthwise, and
thinly sliced

I green serrano chile, finely chopped

2 tablespoons chopped roasted
peanuts

peanut oil or corn oil for frying

In Thailand, this crab cake mixture is typically stuffed into the shells of small blue or mud crabs and deep-fried. Here, it is molded into patties and panfried to make a delicious starter that is paired with a refreshing cucumber salad. Panko, commercially sold Japanese bread crumbs, produce an exceptionally crispy crust.

SERVES 4

✼ In a large bowl, combine the pork, minced shallots, red serrano chile, green onion, bell pepper, 2 tablespoons of the cilantro, 2 tablespoons panko or bread crumbs, fish sauce, pepper, ½ teaspoon of the salt, ¼ teaspoon sugar, and egg. Mix well. If the mixture is too moist and does not hold together, add more panko or bread crumbs. Add the crabmeat and mix without compressing the crab.

✼ Place the 1 cup (4 oz/125 g) panko or bread crumbs in a shallow dish. Scoop up ⅓ cup (3 oz/90 g) crab mixture and form it into a cake 3 inches (7.5 cm) in diameter and ¾ inch (2 cm) thick. Dip each crab cake into the panko or bread crumbs, pressing it into the crumbs and turning to coat both sides. Arrange on a baking sheet. You should have 8 cakes. Loosely cover with plastic wrap and refrigerate for 30 minutes.

✼ Meanwhile, in a small saucepan over medium-high heat, combine the vinegar, 2 tablespoons sugar, and remaining ½ teaspoon salt and bring to a boil. Cook, stirring occasionally, until a light syrup forms, about 5 minutes. Let cool. Place the cucumber, green serrano chile, and sliced shallot in a nonaluminum bowl; add the vinegar mixture, stir gently, and let stand for 15 minutes. Divide the cucumber salad among 4 small plates. Just before serving, sprinkle evenly with the remaining 1 tablespoon cilantro and the peanuts.

✼ In a large frying pan over medium-high heat, pour oil to a depth of ¼ inch (6 mm) and heat until 360°F (182°C) on a deep-frying thermometer. Add the crab cakes without crowding them in the pan and fry, turning once, until crisp and golden brown, 2–3 minutes on each side. Using a slotted spatula, transfer to paper towels to drain.

✼ Serve hot with the cucumber salad.

NUTRITIONAL ANALYSIS PER SERVING: Calories 456 (Kilojoules 1,915); Protein 30 g; Carbohydrates 34 g; Total Fat 22 g; Saturated Fat 5 g; Cholesterol 150 mg; Sodium 1,053 mg; Dietary Fiber 2 g

Chicken Satay with Peanut Sauce

PREP TIME: 1½ HOURS, PLUS
4 HOURS FOR MARINATING

COOKING TIME: 25 MINUTES,
PLUS PREPARING FIRE

INGREDIENTS

5 shallots, quartered

5 cloves garlic, halved

3 red serrano chiles, halved

3 tablespoons finely chopped lemongrass, center white part only

2 tablespoons ground coriander

2 teaspoons granulated sugar

2 teaspoons ground cumin

1½ teaspoons salt

4 tablespoons (2 fl oz/60 ml) water

2 tablespoons unsweetened coconut
cream

8 boneless, skinless chicken thighs,
about 1½ lb (750 g), cut into
1-inch (2.5-cm) pieces

1 piece fresh or frozen galangal,
about 1 inch (2.5 cm), chopped

2 tablespoons peanut or corn oil

¼ cup (2½ oz/75 g) chunky peanut
butter

1 teaspoon palm sugar or brown
sugar

1 teaspoon fish sauce, or to taste

¼ cup (2 fl oz/60 ml) unsweetened
coconut milk, or more as needed

¼ cup (2 fl oz/60 ml) lime juice or
tamarind water (page 111)

1 small cucumber, peeled and thinly
sliced, for garnish

This recipe calls for coconut milk and coconut cream, the rich layer of fat that rises to the top of canned coconut milk. Do not shake the can before opening. Spoon off the layer of cream for the marinade, then stir the remaining milk and use it in the sauce.

SERVES 6

❈ In a blender, combine 2 shallots, 2 garlic cloves, 1 chile, and 2 tablespoons of the lemongrass. Process until finely chopped. Add 1 tablespoon of the coriander, the granulated sugar, 1 teaspoon of the cumin, 1 teaspoon of the salt, and about 2 tablespoons water, just enough to facilitate blending. Process until a smooth paste is formed. Pour into a nonaluminum bowl, add the coconut cream, and mix thoroughly. Add the chicken, turn to coat evenly, cover, and refrigerate for at least 4 hours or as long as overnight.

❈ Prepare a fire in a grill. Position a rack about 2 inches (5 cm) from the heat source. Metal or wooden skewers can be used; if using wooden skewers, soak in water to cover for 20–30 minutes and drain.

❈ In a blender, combine the galangal, remaining 3 shallots, remaining 3 cloves garlic, remaining 2 chiles, remaining 1 tablespoon lemongrass, remaining 1 tablespoon coriander, remaining 1 teaspoon cumin, and about 2 tablespoons water, just enough to facilitate blending. Process until a smooth paste is formed. In a saucepan over medium heat, warm the oil. Add the spice paste and cook, stirring occasionally, until fragrant, about 3 minutes. Add the peanut butter and cook for 2 minutes longer. Stir in the palm or brown sugar, fish sauce, remaining ½ teaspoon salt, and ¼ cup (2 fl oz/60 ml) coconut milk. Cook, stirring occasionally, until beads of oil appear on the surface, about 5 minutes. Stir in the lime juice or tamarind water. Add more coconut milk if needed to make a thick, creamy sauce. Pour into a shallow bowl.

❈ Remove the chicken from the marinade, discarding the marinade. Thread 5 or 6 pieces on each skewer, allowing them to touch. Place directly on the grill rack. Cook, turning once, until the chicken has charred edges, 8–10 minutes. Arrange the skewers on a serving platter, garnish with the cucumber, and accompany with the peanut sauce.

NUTRITIONAL ANALYSIS PER SERVING: Calories 308 (Kilojoules 1,294); Protein 26 g; Carbohydrates 11 g; Total Fat 18 g; Saturated Fat 6 g; Cholesterol 94 mg; Sodium 781 mg; Dietary Fiber 1 g

Squash and Coconut Milk Soup

PREP TIME: 20 MINUTES

COOKING TIME: 25 MINUTES

INGREDIENTS

1 tablespoon dried baby shrimp (prawns)

4 shallots, quartered

2 red or green serrano or jalapeño chiles, seeded

1 stalk lemongrass, center white part only, chopped

2½ cups (20 fl oz/625 ml) unsweetened coconut milk

2 cups (16 fl oz/500 ml) chicken broth or water

6 kaffir lime leaves

1 lb (500 g) kabocha, acorn, or butternut squash, peeled and cut into ¾-inch (2-cm) pieces

1 tablespoon Thai fish sauce

1 tablespoon lime juice

½ teaspoon sugar

½ cup (½ oz/15 g) fresh basil leaves

Thai soups are a complex fusion of spicy, tangy flavors that taste refreshing and light. Here, chunks of squash add texture to broth enriched with coconut milk and seasoned with lemongrass, chiles, lime, and basil.

SERVES 6

❋ Place the dried shrimp in a small bowl, add warm water to cover, and let soak until softened, about 10 minutes. Drain, reserving half of the liquid.

❋ In a blender, combine the shrimp and reserved soaking liquid, shallots, chiles, and lemongrass. Process until a smooth paste forms.

❋ Open the can of coconut milk without shaking it. Scrape the thick cream from the top into a large saucepan over medium-high heat. Stir in the spice paste and bring to a boil. Reduce the heat to medium and cook, stirring occasionally, uncovered, until fragrant, about 5 minutes. Add the remaining coconut milk, chicken broth or water, kaffir lime leaves, and squash and stir. Raise the heat to medium-high and bring to a boil. Reduce the heat to low and simmer, uncovered, stirring once or twice, until the squash is tender, about 15 minutes.

❋ Just before serving, season with the fish sauce, lime juice, sugar, and basil leaves. Taste and adjust the seasonings. Serve hot, ladled into bowls.

NUTRITIONAL ANALYSIS PER SERVING: Calories 235 (Kilojoules 987); Protein 4 g; Carbohydrates 12 g; Total Fat 21 g; Saturated Fat 18 g; Cholesterol 0 mg; Sodium 448 mg; Dietary Fiber 2 g

Sizzling Rice Cake Soup with Crab

PREP TIME: 45 MINUTES

COOKING TIME: 1 HOUR

INGREDIENTS

½ cup (3½ oz/105 g) long-grain rice

½ cup (4 fl oz/125 ml) water

6 dried Chinese black mushrooms, soaked in warm water for 20 minutes, then drained

1 tablespoon peanut oil, plus oil for frying

1 teaspoon salt

4 water chestnuts, cut into ¼-inch (6-mm) dice

½ cup (2½ oz/75 g) drained, canned bamboo shoots, cut into ¼-inch (6-mm) dice

¼ cup (2 fl oz/60 ml) Chinese rice wine or dry sherry

6 cups (48 fl oz/1.5 l) chicken broth

1 tablespoon light soy sauce

large pinch of ground white pepper

large pinch of sugar

3 tablespoons cornstarch (cornflour) mixed with ¼ cup (2 fl oz/60 ml) water

½ cup (2½ oz/75 g) frozen petite peas, thawed

½ lb (250 g) firm tofu, finely diced

¼ lb (125 g) cooked fresh crabmeat, flaked

1 green (spring) onion, including tender green tops, chopped

SERVES 6

❀ Place the rice in a fine-mesh sieve and rinse under cold running water until the water runs clear; drain thoroughly. In an 8-inch (20-cm) frying pan over medium-high heat, combine the rice and water and bring to a boil, stirring to loosen the grains from the pan bottom. Cook until the surface water is completely absorbed, about 5 minutes. Reduce the heat to low, cover, and cook until the rice is glistening white, about 15 minutes. Uncover and continue to cook until it shrinks from the pan sides and forms a hard, dry crust, about 15 minutes. It should be easy to lift from the pan with a spatula; if not, continue to cook. Let cool, then break into irregular 2-inch (5-cm) pieces.

❀ Remove the stems from the mushrooms and discard. Finely dice the caps. Heat a large saucepan over medium-high heat. Add the 1 tablespoon oil, salt, mushrooms, water chestnuts, and bamboo shoots and toss and stir for 30 seconds. Pour in the rice wine or sherry and cook until the alcohol evaporates, about 15 seconds. Add the broth, soy sauce, white pepper, and sugar, stir well, and bring to a boil. Add the cornstarch mixture, stirring continuously, and cook until thickened, about 30 seconds. Remove from the heat, cover, and keep warm.

❀ Preheat an oven to 425°F (220°C). Line a baking sheet with paper towels. In a saucepan over medium-high heat, pour oil to a depth of 2 inches (5 cm) and heat until 375°F (190°C) on a deep-frying thermometer. Working in batches, add the rice cakes to the hot oil. Fry until puffed up and doubled in size, about 5 seconds. (If the rice cakes do not puff in the oil within 10 seconds, the oil is not hot enough or the cakes are not completely bone-dry.) Using tongs, turn and fry until golden brown, about 10 seconds. Transfer to the paper towels to drain, then place on a heatproof plate and keep hot in the oven. Just before the last batch is fried, bring the soup to a boil over high heat and add the peas and tofu. Transfer to a tureen and add the crabmeat and green onion.

❀ Bring the soup to the table and immediately add the hot rice cakes. They should sizzle on contact. Ladle into bowls and serve at once.

NUTRITIONAL ANALYSIS PER SERVING: Calories 277 (Kilojoules 1,163); Protein 12 g; Carbohydrates 26 g; Total Fat 13 g; Saturated Fat 2 g; Cholesterol 19 mg; Sodium 1,565 mg; Dietary Fiber 2 g

Spicy Stuffed Omelet Pouches

PREP TIME: 30 MINUTES

COOKING TIME: 25 MINUTES

INGREDIENTS

FOR THE FILLING

1 tablespoon peanut or corn oil

3 cloves garlic, minced

1 small yellow onion, finely chopped

1 red serrano or jalapeño chile, seeded and chopped

½ lb (250 g) ground (minced) chicken

¼ lb (125 g) green beans, trimmed and cut into ¼-inch (6-mm) pieces

2 tablespoons Thai fish sauce

1 tablespoon palm sugar or brown sugar

¼ teaspoon ground pepper

1 tomato, coarsely chopped

⅓ cup (⅓ oz/10 g) coarsely chopped fresh cilantro (fresh coriander)

FOR THE OMELETS

4 eggs

2 tablespoons water

1½ teaspoons Thai fish sauce

2 teaspoons peanut or corn oil

4 sprigs fresh cilantro (fresh coriander)

Sriracha sauce or Thai fish sauce (optional)

Here, a thin omelet with a rich, tasty filling of chicken, green beans, tomatoes, and chile is shaped into a pouch. It is perfect served as a first course with Striped Bass Grilled in Banana Leaves (page 69).

SERVES 4

❁ Preheat an oven to 250°F (120°C).

❁ To make the filling, in a wok over medium-high heat, warm the oil. Add the garlic, onion, and chile and toss and stir until the onion is golden, 2–3 minutes. Raise the heat to high, add the chicken, and stir to break up any large clumps. Continue tossing and stirring until the chicken is crumbled and dry, 3–5 minutes. Add the green beans, fish sauce, sugar, and pepper and toss and stir for 2 minutes longer. Add the tomato and toss and stir until the mixture thickens, about 3 minutes. Remove from the heat and stir in the cilantro. Transfer to a bowl and set aside.

❁ To make the omelets, in a bowl, whisk the eggs, water, and fish sauce. In a 10-inch (25-cm) frying pan over medium-high heat, warm ½ teaspoon of the oil and swirl to spread it over the pan bottom. Pour in ⅓ cup (3 fl oz/80 ml) of the egg mixture, tilting the pan to spread it evenly over the pan bottom. Cook until brown and the edges begin to shrink from the pan sides, about 1 minute. With the tip of a spatula, lift the edges, slip the spatula underneath the omelet, turn the omelet, and continue to cook until the second side is brown, about 30 seconds. Transfer to a flat surface, placing the well-browned side down.

❁ Spoon ½ cup (4 oz/125 g) of the filling in the center. Fold 2 opposite sides so they overlap in the center. Fold in the remaining sides to enclose the filling and form a square. Transfer, seam side down, to a serving plate. Using a sharp knife, make 3 cuts at right angles in the top of the omelet to form a square, leaving 1 side uncut. Lift the square to expose the filling. Garnish with a cilantro sprig and a swirl of Sriracha or Thai fish sauce, if desired. Loosely cover the omelet with aluminum foil and keep warm in the oven until ready to serve. Repeat to make the 3 remaining omelet pouches. Serve immediately.

NUTRITIONAL ANALYSIS PER SERVING: Calories 280 (Kilojoules 1,176); Protein 19 g; Carbohydrates 13 g; Total Fat 17 g; Saturated Fat 4 g; Cholesterol 260 mg; Sodium 491 mg; Dietary Fiber 2 g

Grilled Shrimp Mousse on Sugarcane Sticks

PREP TIME: 45 MINUTES

COOKING TIME: 10 MINUTES,
PLUS PREPARING FIRE

INGREDIENTS

2 large shallots, quartered

2 cloves garlic

I green (spring) onion, white part
only, chopped

I tablespoon fish sauce

I teaspoon sugar

I teaspoon cornstarch (cornflour)

½ teaspoon salt

¼ teaspoon ground pepper

I lb (500 g) medium shrimp
(prawns), peeled, deveined, and
patted dry

2 egg whites, beaten until frothy

3 pieces fresh or canned sugarcane,
about 6 inches (15 cm) long,
quartered lengthwise

12 red-leaf or butter (Boston)
lettuce leaves

12 sprigs fresh cilantro (fresh
coriander)

36 mint leaves

I small English (hothouse)
cucumber, halved lengthwise and
thinly sliced

Garlic-Lime Dipping Sauce *(page 61)*

Sugarcane skewers are wrapped with shrimp mousse, steamed, and then grilled until toasty brown. The hot shrimp is pulled off the sugarcane, wrapped in a lettuce leaf with cilantro, mint, and cucumber, and enjoyed with dipping sauce. For this Vietnamese starter, you can also use lemongrass stalks, cut to 6 inches (15 cm) long and ¼ inch (6 mm) wide, as skewers.

SERVES 6

❊ In a food processor, combine the shallots, garlic, and green onion and process until finely minced. Add the fish sauce, sugar, cornstarch, salt, and pepper; pulse once or twice to mix. Add the shrimp and process until puréed, 5–10 seconds. Scrape down the sides of the bowl and add the egg whites; pulse a few times to combine.

❊ Oil a baking sheet. With wet hands, shape 2 tablespoons of the shrimp purée into an oblong ball. Mold around the middle of a length of sugarcane, leaving 1½ inches (4 cm) uncovered at each end. Set on the prepared sheet. Repeat with the remaining shrimp purée and sugarcane.

❊ Prepare a fire in a grill. Arrange the lettuce leaves, cilantro sprigs, mint leaves, and cucumber slices on a serving platter.

❊ Bring a wok half full of water to a boil. Oil the bottom of a bamboo steam basket or a heatproof plate. Arrange the sugarcane sticks in the basket or on the plate without touching. Set in the wok, cover, and cook until the shrimp is opaque, 4–5 minutes. If using a plate, pat the sugarcane sticks with paper towels to remove excess moisture.

❊ When the coals are hot, oil the grill rack, set the sticks diagonally across the rack, and grill, turning occasionally, until golden brown, 3–5 minutes.

❊ Transfer to the serving platter and serve immediately. Wrap a lettuce leaf around the shrimp and carefully remove from the sugarcane stick. Add a cilantro sprig, 3 mint leaves, and several cucumber slices. Roll up the lettuce to enclose the mixture and dip in the sauce. Chew on the sugarcane in between bites of shrimp.

NUTRITIONAL ANALYSIS PER SERVING: Calories 100 (Kilojoules 420); Protein 15 g; Carbohydrates 6 g; Total Fat 1 g; Saturated Fat 0 g; Cholesterol 93 mg; Sodium 405 mg; Dietary Fiber 1 g

California Rolls

PREP TIME: 1½ HOURS

COOKING TIME: 40 MINUTES

INGREDIENTS

3½ cups (1½ lb/750 g) short-
grain rice

3¾ cups (30 fl oz/940 ml) cold
water

⅓ cup (3 fl oz/80 ml) plus 1½ tablespoons water

2 teaspoons plus ½ cup (4 fl oz/125 ml)
unseasoned rice vinegar

2 tablespoons wasabi powder

⅓ cup (3 oz/90 g) sugar

1 teaspoon salt

6 sheets toasted nori seaweed,
about 7 by 8 inches (18 by 20 cm)

¼ cup (1 oz/30 g) sesame seeds,
toasted in a dry frying pan for 3–5
minutes

¾ English (hothouse) cucumber,
peeled and cut into thin strips
6 inches (15 cm) long

1½ avocadoes, pitted, peeled, and
cut into slices ¼ inch (6 mm) thick

6 oz (185 g) cooked fresh crabmeat,
flaked into pieces

½ cup (4 fl oz/125 ml) Japanese soy
sauce for dipping

¾ cup (5 oz/155 g) pickled ginger
slices

SERVES 6

✲ Place the rice in a bowl and wash with cold water until the water runs clear. Drain and place in a 3-qt (3-l) saucepan with the 3¾ cups (30 fl oz/940 ml) cold water. Bring to a boil. Cook, uncovered, stirring occasionally, until all the surface water is absorbed, about 3 minutes. Cover, reduce the heat to low, and cook, without stirring, until tender, about 20 minutes. Set aside for 10 minutes.

✲ In a small bowl, combine the ⅓ cup (3 fl oz/80 ml) water and 2 tea-spoons vinegar. In another small bowl, combine the wasabi powder and 1½ tablespoons water, stir to form a smooth paste, and let stand for 10 minutes. Divide in half and set half aside. In a small saucepan over low heat, combine the ½ cup (4 oz/125 ml) vinegar, the sugar, and the salt and cook, stirring occasionally, until the sugar and salt are dissolved, about 3 minutes. Set aside to cool.

✲ Transfer the hot rice to a large bowl. Drizzle with two-thirds of the vinegar-sugar mixture and gently fold into the rice. Add only as much as the rice will absorb without becoming mushy. Cover with a damp kitchen towel.

✲ Place a bamboo sushi mat on a work surface with the bamboo strips running horizontally. Place 1 nori sheet horizontally, shiny side down, on the mat, aligned with the edge nearest you. Dip your hands into the vinegar-water mixture and spread about 2 cups (10 oz/315 g) of the rice in an even layer over the nori sheet, leaving the top one-fourth uncov-ered. Smear a thin strip of wasabi horizontally across the middle. Sprinkle with sesame seeds over the wasabi, followed by a few cucumber strips, an even row of avocado slices, and one-sixth of the crabmeat. Following the instructions on page 12, form a snug cylinder about 2 inches (5 cm) wide. Dipping a sharp knife in water before each cut, cut the roll in half. Cut each half into 4 equal pieces. Repeat with the remaining 5 nori sheets.

✲ Serve the sushi with the reserved wasabi, the soy sauce, and the pickled ginger. Provide small dishes for mixing a small amount of wasabi with soy sauce for use as a dipping sauce.

NUTRITIONAL ANALYSIS PER SERVING: Calories 509 (Kilojoules 2,138); Protein 13 g; Carbohydrates 95 g; Total Fat 9 g; Saturated Fat 1 g; Cholesterol 21 mg; Sodium 1,488 mg; Dietary Fiber 2 g

Spicy Asparagus Bean Salad

PREP TIME: 50 MINUTES

COOKING TIME: 30 MINUTES

INGREDIENTS

1 tablespoon vegetable oil

6 oz (185 g) ground (minced) dark-meat chicken

3 tablespoons grated unsweetened coconut

½ lb (250 g) asparagus beans or slender green beans such as Blue Lake, trimmed

¼ lb (125 g) cooked shrimp (prawns), cut into ¼-inch (6-mm) pieces

½ red bell pepper (capsicum), cut into ¼-inch (6-mm) dice

1 red serrano chile, seeded and chopped

1 green serrano chile, seeded and chopped

FOR THE GARLIC AND SHALLOT CHIPS

2 cups (16 fl oz/500 ml) peanut or corn oil for frying

6 shallots, about 6 oz (185 g), cut into thin slivers

8 cloves garlic, cut into thin slivers

FOR THE DRESSING

¼ cup (2 fl oz/60 ml) lime juice

1 tablespoon Thai roasted chile paste

1 tablespoon fish sauce

1 tablespoon sugar

4 tablespoons (2 fl oz/60 ml) coconut cream (page 103)

3 tablespoons roasted peanuts, chopped, for garnish

This hearty salad is ideal for potlucks and outdoor summer buffets. The flavors intensify when all the chopped ingredients are mixed and dressed ahead of serving. Chinese asparagus beans, also known as yard-long beans, replace winged beans, which are used in the classic Thai preparation.

SERVES 6

✻ In a small frying pan over medium-high heat, warm the 1 tablespoon oil. Add the chicken and sauté, breaking up any clumps, until opaque and crumbly, about 5 minutes. Transfer to a large bowl.

✻ In a small dry frying pan over medium heat, toast the coconut, stirring occasionally, until golden brown, about 5 minutes. Bring a saucepan three-fourths full of water to a boil. Add the beans and blanch until tender-crisp, about 1 minute. Drain and rinse under cold running water to halt the cooking. Cut into ¼-inch (6-mm) pieces. Add the grated coconut, beans, shrimp, bell pepper, and chiles to the chicken and stir to combine.

✻ To make the garlic and shallot chips, in a small 8½-inch (21.5-cm) frying pan over medium heat, warm the 2 cups (16 fl oz/500 ml) peanut or corn oil until the temperature reaches 325°F (165°C) on a deep-frying thermometer. Add the shallots and fry until golden brown and crisp, 5–8 minutes. Using a slotted spoon, transfer to paper towels to drain. Add the garlic to the heated oil and fry until golden brown and crisp, 5–8 minutes. Transfer to paper towels to drain.

✻ To make the dressing, in a bowl, combine the lime juice, chile paste, fish sauce, and sugar. Whisk in 3 tablespoons of the coconut cream.

✻ Pour the dressing over the salad, add the garlic and shallot chips, and toss gently to combine. Transfer to a platter. Drizzle with the remaining 1 tablespoon coconut cream and garnish with the peanuts. Serve at once.

NUTRITIONAL ANALYSIS PER SERVING: Calories 222 (Kilojoules 932); Protein 13 g; Carbohydrates 15 g; Total Fat 13 g; Saturated Fat 5 g; Cholesterol 60 mg; Sodium 287 mg; Dietary Fiber 2 g

Vegetable Stir-Fry with Bean Thread Noodles

PREP TIME: 45 MINUTES, PLUS
20 MINUTES FOR SOAKING

COOKING TIME: 10 MINUTES

INGREDIENTS

6 dried Chinese black mushrooms

1½ oz (45 g) dried bean thread
vermicelli noodles

¼ cup (1 oz/30 g) dried lily buds
(optional)

¼ cup (1 oz/30 g) dried tree ear
mushrooms (optional)

2 tablespoons vegetable oil

2 cloves garlic, sliced lengthwise

¼ head green cabbage, cut into
1-inch (2.5-cm) pieces

¼ lb (125 g) green beans, trimmed
and cut on the diagonal into
1½-inch (4-cm) pieces

1½ cups (3 oz/90 g) small cauliflower
florets

1 carrot, peeled and cut on the
diagonal into thin slices

1 tablespoon preserved red bean
curd or 2 tablespoons oyster sauce

1–1½ cups (8–12 fl oz/250–375 ml)
water

1 tablespoon soy sauce

1 teaspoon sugar

½ teaspoon salt

This hearty and earthy-tasting vegetable stir-fry is an everyday variation of a vegetarian dish served on Chinese New Year, in reverence to Buddha. The combination of dried and fresh vegetables produces an extraordinary fusion of flavors that is absorbed by the bean thread noodles.

SERVES 4–6

✹ Place the black mushrooms in a bowl, add water to cover, and soak until softened, about 20 minutes. Drain. Remove the stems and discard. Cut the caps into ½-inch (12-mm) slices and set aside. Place the noodles in another bowl, add warm water to cover, and soak until soft and pliable, about 20 minutes. Drain. Using kitchen scissors, make 3 or 4 cuts in the mound of noodles and set aside.

✹ If using the lily buds, place in a small bowl, add warm water to cover, and soak until softened, about 5 minutes. Drain and squeeze out the excess water. Cut off the hard root ends and discard. Set the lily buds aside. If using the tree ear mushrooms, place in another bowl, add warm water to cover, and let stand until tripled in size, about 5 minutes. Drain and rinse off any sand or grit. Set aside.

✹ Place a wok over medium-high heat. Add the oil and garlic and cook until the garlic is golden, about 30 seconds. Add the black mushrooms, lily buds, and tree ear mushrooms and toss and stir for 30 seconds. Add the cabbage, green beans, cauliflower, and carrot and toss and stir for 1 minute. Push the vegetables to the side of the wok and add the preserved bean curd or oyster sauce, 1 cup (8 fl oz/250 ml) of the water, soy sauce, sugar, salt, and noodles and toss with the vegetables. Cover and simmer until the vegetables are tender-crisp, the noodles are tender and plump, and the liquid is fully absorbed, about 3 minutes. If the mixture becomes too dry before the vegetables are cooked, add more water.

✹ Serve hot.

NUTRITIONAL ANALYSIS PER SERVING: Calories 120 (Kilojoules 504); Protein 2 g; Carbohydrates 16 g; Total Fat 6 g; Saturated Fat 1 g; Cholesterol 0 mg; Sodium 599 mg; Dietary Fiber 3 g

Grilled Eggplant with Mung Bean Noodles

PREP TIME: 40 MINUTES,
PLUS 1 HOUR FOR CHILLING

COOKING TIME: 20 MINUTES,
PLUS PREPARING FIRE

INGREDIENTS

2 oz (60 g) dried mung bean
noodles

4 Asian (slender) eggplants
(aubergines), about 6 inches
(15 cm) long, or 1 globe eggplant,
about 1¼ lb (625 g)

peanut oil for brushing

FOR THE DRESSING

2 tablespoons peanut oil

3 cloves garlic, finely minced

1 piece fresh ginger, about 1 inch
(2.5 cm) long, peeled and grated

2 green (spring) onions, including
tender green tops, minced

¼ cup (2 fl oz/60 ml) dark soy sauce
or Japanese soy sauce

3 tablespoons red wine vinegar or
balsamic vinegar

1½ tablespoons Asian sesame oil

1 teaspoon hot chili oil, or to taste

1 teaspoon sugar

½ teaspoon salt

1 tablespoon sesame seeds

1 small English (hothouse) cucumber,
peeled and cut into thin strips
2 inches (5 cm) long

1 green (spring) onion, including
tender green tops, minced

2 tablespoons coarsely chopped
fresh cilantro (fresh coriander)

Traditionally, the eggplants for this Sichuan salad are steamed before being torn into shreds. Here, they are grilled, which gives depth to their flavor. The dried mung bean noodles, also called glass noodles, sold in Asian markets and well-stocked food stores, are fine and transparent when cooked, hence their alternative names: glass, cellophane, mirror, and transparent noodles.

SERVES 4

❀ Place the noodles in a bowl, add water to cover, and soak until soft and pliable, about 15 minutes. Drain. Bring a large pot three-fourths full of water to a boil. Add the noodles and cook until plump and as clear as glass, about 3 minutes. Drain, refresh with cold water, and drain again. Using kitchen scissors, make 4 or 5 cuts in the mound of noodles. Place in a large bowl, cover, and refrigerate for about 30 minutes.

❀ Prepare a fire in a grill.

❀ Cut the eggplants lengthwise into slices ¼ inch (6 mm) thick. Brush both sides with peanut oil. When the coals are hot, place the slices directly on the grill rack. Cook, turning once, until tender and marked with grill lines, about 2 minutes per side. Remove to a plate. Let cool, then cut into strips 2 inches (5 cm) long. Transfer to a bowl, cover, and refrigerate for about 30 minutes.

❀ Meanwhile, make the dressing: In a small saucepan over medium heat, combine the peanut oil, garlic, and ginger. Sauté, without browning, until aromatic, about 1 minute. Remove from the heat, add the green onions, soy sauce, vinegar, sesame oil, chili oil, sugar, and salt and stir to combine. Pour the dressing over the eggplant and mix well.

❀ In a small dry frying pan over low heat, toast the sesame seeds, stirring occasionally, until fragrant, 3–5 minutes.

❀ Add the cucumber strips, green onion, and cilantro to the chilled noodles. If the noodles stick, add just enough cold water to separate them and drain before tossing. Scatter with the chilled eggplant strips. Sprinkle with the sesame seeds. Serve chilled.

NUTRITIONAL ANALYSIS PER SERVING: Calories 309 (Kilojoules 1,298); Protein 4 g; Carbohydrates 29 g; Total Fat 21 g; Saturated Fat 3 g; Cholesterol 0 mg; Sodium 1,619 mg; Dietary Fiber 3 g

Green Papaya and Carrot Salad with Roasted Peanuts

PREP TIME: 30 MINUTES

INGREDIENTS

1½ lb (750 g) green papaya, daikon, or jicama

1 carrot, peeled

ice water as needed

FOR THE DRESSING

1 small red chile, chopped

1 clove garlic, finely minced

1 tablespoon sugar

2 tablespoons Vietnamese fish sauce

1½ tablespoons lime juice with pulp

1½ tablespoons unseasoned rice vinegar

2 red jalapeño chiles, seeded and finely sliced

3 tablespoons chopped fresh cilantro (fresh coriander)

2 tablespoons chopped fresh Vietnamese mint

¼ cup (1 oz/30 g) chopped roasted peanuts, for garnish

6 shrimp (prawn) chips, for garnish

PREP TIP: If you do not have a mandoline, you can use a sharp knife or a food processor fitted with a shredding disk to cut the papaya, daikon, or jicama and the carrot into julienne strips.

The mild tart flavor and crunchy texture of green papaya highlight this Vietnamese salad dressed with a spicy lime vinaigrette. Green papaya, a large immature cousin of the common papaya, is available whole and preshredded in Asian markets. Also look in Asian markets for packages of shrimp chips.

SERVES 6

If using green papaya, cut in half lengthwise, peel, and scrape out and discard the seeds. Using a mandoline fitted with the thin julienne slicing blade, shred into julienne strips no wider than ⅛ inch (3 mm). If using daikon or jicama, peel and shred in the same manner. Shred the carrot into julienne strips. Place the shredded papaya, daikon, or jicama in a bowl of ice water. Add the carrot and let stand until crisp, about 10 minutes.

Meanwhile, prepare the dressing: Place the chile, garlic, and sugar in a mini food processor and process until a loose paste is formed. Alternatively, place in a mortar and grind with a pestle. Transfer to a bowl and add the fish sauce, lime juice, and vinegar and stir to combine.

Drain the papaya, daikon, or jicama and the carrot. Pat dry and place in a large bowl. Add the jalapeño chiles, cilantro, and mint. Pour the dressing over the salad and toss to coat the ingredients evenly. Let stand to absorb the flavors for at least 10 minutes or up to 1 hour.

To serve, use tongs to pick up portions of the salad and shake gently to drain any excess liquid clinging to the salad. Arrange on individual plates, garnish with the peanuts, and accompany with shrimp chips.

NUTRITIONAL ANALYSIS PER SERVING: Calories 88 (Kilojoules 370); Protein 3 g; Carbohydrates 14 g; Total Fat 3 g; Saturated Fat 1 g; Cholesterol 0 mg; Sodium 245 mg; Dietary Fiber 2 g

Spicy Fried Noodles with Tomatoes and Cabbage

PREP TIME: 1 HOUR

COOKING TIME: 15 MINUTES

INGREDIENTS

½ lb (250 g) Hokkien noodles or
  thick Chinese-style egg noodles

3 tablespoons peanut oil

3 cloves garlic, chopped

1 yellow onion, sliced

6 oz (185 g) large shrimp (prawns),
  peeled, deveined, and halved
  lengthwise

1 small carrot, peeled and julienned

¼ lb (125 g) red cabbage, cut into
  ¾-inch (2-cm) cubes

3 green (spring) onions, including
  tender green tops, cut into 1-inch
  (2.5-cm) pieces

3 small firm tomatoes, cut into
  ½-inch (12-mm) cubes

1 boiled potato, peeled and cut into
  ¾-inch (2-cm) cubes

3 tablespoons tomato ketchup or
  tomato paste

1 tablespoon chili sauce

1 tablespoon kecap manis

1 tablespoon soy sauce

1 teaspoon sugar

2 eggs

1 green chile, sliced

1 small English (hothouse)
  cucumber, sliced

1 lemon, cut lengthwise into 4 wedges

This popular Indonesian fried noodle dish, called *mee goreng,* reflects the cross-cultural influences prevalent throughout Southeast Asia. Thick egg noodles are fried with tomato ketchup and tomatoes, potatoes, and cabbage—Western vegetables adopted by Indonesians. *Kecap manis* is an Indonesian sweet soy sauce sold in Southeast Asian markets.

SERVES 4

❀ If using Hokkien noodles, rinse with warm water; set aside. If using Chinese-style egg noodles, bring a large pot three-fourths full of water to a boil. Add the noodles, stir to loosen the strands, return to a boil, and cook until tender, about 1 minute. Drain, rinse thoroughly with cold running water, and drain again. Set aside.

❀ In a nonstick wok over high heat, warm 2 tablespoons of the oil. Add the garlic and yellow onion and toss and stir until lightly browned, about 2 minutes. Add the shrimp and toss and stir until bright orange, about 1 minute. Add the carrot, cabbage, and green onions and toss and stir until the vegetables begin to wilt, about 1 minute. Add the tomatoes and potato and toss and stir, being careful not to break up the cubes, until heated, 1–2 minutes. Transfer to a plate and set aside.

❀ Return the wok to high heat and add the remaining 1 tablespoon oil. Add the noodles and toss to lightly coat with the oil. Add the ketchup or tomato paste, chili sauce, kecap manis, soy sauce, and sugar and toss to thoroughly coat the noodles, about 2 minutes.

❀ Push the noodles up the side of the wok to make a well in the middle. Crack the eggs into the well and lightly beat. Cook, without stirring, until set, about 1 minute. Gently fold the eggs into the noodles. Add the reserved vegetables and stir to combine.

❀ Divide among individual bowls. Top with the green chile and cucumber slices and accompany with the lemon wedges.

NUTRITIONAL ANALYSIS PER SERVING: Calories 500 (Kilojoules 2,100); Protein 22 g; Carbohydrates 71 g; Total Fat 16 g; Saturated Fat 3 g; Cholesterol 213 mg; Sodium 736 mg; Dietary Fiber 6 g

Buckwheat Noodles with Dipping Sauce

PREP TIME: 25 MINUTES, PLUS
1 HOUR FOR CHILLING

COOKING TIME: 15 MINUTES

INGREDIENTS

FOR THE DIPPING SAUCE
1 piece kombu seaweed, about
    3 inches (7.5 cm) long

3 cups (24 fl oz/750 ml) water

½ cup (4 fl oz/125 ml) soy sauce

¼ cup (2 fl oz/60 ml) mirin

1 teaspoon sugar

3½ cups (1¾ oz/50 g) loosely
    packed bonito flakes

¾ lb (375 g) dried buckwheat noodles

2 tablespoons wasabi powder

4½ teaspoons water

6 green (spring) onions, including
    tender green tops, minced

¼ cup (¼ oz/7 g) finely shredded
    toasted nori seaweed

6 tablespoons grated daikon

PREP TIP: Each diner uses chopsticks
to mix a dab of wasabi with the
green onions or daikon, smears
them on the noodles, then dips the
noodles into the dipping sauce.

This Japanese noodle dish, *zaru soba*, is traditionally presented in slatted bamboo boxes or baskets to ensure perfectly drained noodles. Using flat soup bowls makes an equally elegant presentation. The buckwheat noodles, called soba, are dipped into a delicately seasoned sauce and served with the Japanese horseradish called wasabi, for a spicy kick; tiny mounds of grated daikon, a sweet, crisp radish; and finely chopped green onions. Nori is available already toasted and shredded.

SERVES 6

❋ To make the dipping sauce, using a damp kitchen towel, wipe, but do not wash, the kombu. In a saucepan over medium heat, combine the kombu and the water. Slowly bring almost to a boil, then remove the kombu. Return the water to a boil over medium-high heat, add the soy sauce, mirin, and sugar, and bring just to a boil. Add the bonito flakes; do not stir. Immediately remove from the heat and let stand until the flakes sink to the bottom of the pan, about 10 minutes. Pour through a fine-mesh sieve into a bowl. Cover and refrigerate for 1 hour or for up to 2 days.

❋ Bring a large pot three-fourths full of water to a boil. Add the noodles, stirring to separate the strands, and bring to a boil. Reduce the heat to medium-high and cook, stirring occasionally, until tender but firm to the bite, 3–5 minutes or according to the package directions. Drain, rinse thoroughly with cold running water, and divide among 6 bowls. Cover and set aside.

❋ In a small bowl, combine the wasabi powder and water. Stir to form a smooth paste and set aside for 10 minutes. Rinse the green onions under cold running water and gently squeeze to remove excess moisture and any bitter flavor.

❋ To serve, sprinkle the shredded nori over the noodles, dividing evenly. Pour the dipping sauce into 6 small bowls. Arrange equal amounts of wasabi, green onions, and daikon in 6 small condiment dishes.

NUTRITIONAL ANALYSIS PER SERVING: Calories 290 (Kilojoules 1,218); Protein 20 g; Carbohydrates 51 g; Total Fat 1 g; Saturated Fat 0 g; Cholesterol 25 mg; Sodium 3,005 mg; Dietary Fiber 3 g

Chile Fried Rice with Crab and Thai Basil

PREP TIME: 30 MINUTES

COOKING TIME: 10 MINUTES

INGREDIENTS

2 tablespoons vegetable oil

2 shallots, finely chopped

3 cloves garlic, finely chopped

½ teaspoon salt

4 cups (20 oz/625 g) cooked
long-grain rice, chilled

1–2 tablespoons Thai fish sauce,
or to taste

1 tablespoon soy sauce

½ teaspoon sugar

2 eggs

3 green (spring) onions, including
1 inch (2.5 cm) tender green tops,
chopped

2 red serrano chiles, finely chopped

½ cup (½ oz/15 g) fresh Thai basil
leaves or sweet basil leaves

¼ lb (125 g) cooked fresh crabmeat,
flaked

COOKING TIP: Cold leftover rice
makes the best fried rice. Asian
cooks often make extra rice for the
evening meal just to have leftovers
for fried rice in the morning.

Thai fried rice, a variation of the basic Chinese fried rice, is made
with generous amounts of garlic, shallots, chiles, and Thai basil.
A sprinkling of fish sauce, the soy sauce of Thai cooking, gives
this dish a special twist.

SERVES 4–6

✸ Warm a wok over medium-high heat. Add 1 tablespoon of the oil and
tilt the wok to coat the entire surface. Add the shallots and cook until
golden brown, about 1 minute. Remove to paper towels to drain.

✸ Return the wok to medium-high heat and add the remaining 1 tablespoon oil, tilting the wok to coat the surface. Add the garlic and salt and
cook until the garlic is golden brown, about 1 minute. Raise the heat
to high, break up any clumps of rice, add to the wok, and toss and stir
until the grains are separated, about 2 minutes. Add the fish sauce, soy
sauce, and sugar and toss and stir until the grains are evenly seasoned,
about 30 seconds.

✸ Push the rice up the sides of the wok to make a well in the center.
Crack the eggs into the well, lightly beat, and cook, without stirring,
until set, about 30 seconds. Gently fold the eggs into the rice until
specks of cooked egg appear throughout the grains. Add the green
onions, chiles, basil, and crabmeat and toss to mix thoroughly.

✸ Transfer to a serving dish, top with the reserved shallots, and serve
at once.

NUTRITIONAL ANALYSIS PER SERVING: Calories 274 (Kilojoules 1,151); Protein 12 g;
Carbohydrates 36 g; Total Fat 9 g; Saturated Fat 2 g; Cholesterol 108 mg; Sodium 708 mg;
Dietary Fiber 1 g

Pad Thai

PREP TIME: 45 MINUTES

COOKING TIME: 15 MINUTES

INGREDIENTS

½ lb (250 g) dried rice ribbon noodles

2 tablespoons vegetable oil, or as needed

1 skinless, boneless chicken breast half, about ¼ lb (125 g), cut into strips ⅛ inch (3 mm) thick

¼ lb (125 g) medium shrimp (prawns), peeled and deveined

3 cloves garlic, minced

¼ cup (1½ oz/45 g) minced shallot or yellow onion

3 tablespoons tomato ketchup or tomato paste

2 tablespoons plus 1½ teaspoons Thai fish sauce

2 tablespoons lime juice or rice vinegar

1 tablespoon sugar

1 egg

large pinch of red pepper flakes

4 tablespoons (2 fl oz/60 ml) chicken broth

½ lb (250 g) mung bean sprouts

6 green (spring) onions, including tender green tops, cut into 2-inch (5-cm) pieces

1 carrot, peeled and julienned

⅓ cup (2½ oz/75 g) chopped roasted peanuts

½ cup (½ oz/15 g) fresh cilantro (fresh coriander) leaves

1 lime, cut into 6 wedges

This simple home-style noodle dish made with chicken and shrimp is quick and easy to prepare. The right noodle is essential. Look in Asian markets and well-stocked food stores for the flat ribbon-shaped noodle called *sen lek* in Thai. They are ⅛ inch (3 mm) wide and made with rice flour.

SERVES 6

❋ Place the noodles in a bowl, add warm water to cover, and soak until soft and pliable, about 15 minutes. Drain and set aside.

❋ In a nonstick wok over medium-high heat, warm 1 tablespoon of the oil. Add the chicken and toss and stir until opaque, about 1 minute. Add the shrimp and toss and stir until bright pink, about 1 minute longer. Transfer to a bowl and set aside.

❋ Return the wok to medium-high heat and add the remaining 1 tablespoon oil. Add the garlic and shallot or onion and toss and stir until golden, about 1 minute. Raise the heat to high and add the ketchup or tomato paste, fish sauce, lime juice or rice vinegar, and sugar. Toss and stir until thickened, about 30 seconds. Break the egg into the middle of the wok, lightly beat, and cook, without stirring, until set, about 20 seconds. Gently fold the egg into the sauce; tiny egg flecks should peek through the sauce. Add the noodles and red pepper flakes, and, using tongs, toss to coat with the sauce. Add the chicken broth, 2 tablespoons at a time, to moisten the stiff noodles, and cook until the noodles begin to cling together and are almost tender, about 3 minutes. Add the bean sprouts, green onions, carrot, chicken-shrimp mixture, and half of the peanuts. Toss to combine and cook until the bean sprouts begin to wilt, about 3 minutes.

❋ Divide among individual plates and top with the remaining peanuts and the cilantro. Squeeze the lime wedges over the noodles. Serve hot or at room temperature.

NUTRITIONAL ANALYSIS PER SERVING: Calories 354 (Kilojoules 1,487); Protein 14 g; Carbohydrates 48 g; Total Fat 13 g; Saturated Fat 2 g; Cholesterol 69 mg; Sodium 599 mg; Dietary Fiber 2 g

Tangy Mango Relish

PREP TIME: 20 MINUTES, PLUS
20 MINUTES FOR STANDING

COOKING TIME: 3 MINUTES

INGREDIENTS

2 red jalapeño chiles, seeded

¼ cup (2 fl oz/60 ml) water

3 tablespoons white vinegar

4 teaspoons sugar

½ teaspoon salt

1 large firm mango, peeled and cut
into ¾-inch (2-cm) cubes

1 tablespoon lime juice

1 tablespoon coarsely chopped
fresh mint

1 tablespoon coarsely chopped
fresh cilantro (fresh coriander)

Side dishes, a multitude of them, are integral to a Malaysian meal. The relishes, pickles, chutneys, and salads add breadth and sparkle to the immense range of flavors in Malaysian dishes. Called *kerabu,* this side dish is more like a salad relish. It is just the right tonic for hot spicy dishes.

SERVES 8

✺ Place the chiles and the water in a food processor or blender and process until coarsely puréed, leaving small bits of chile. Transfer to a small saucepan and add the vinegar, sugar, and salt. Cook over medium heat, stirring occasionally, until the sugar dissolves, about 3 minutes. Let cool.

✺ Add the mango, lime juice, mint, and cilantro and stir gently to combine. Cover and let stand at room temperature until the flavors meld, about 20 minutes, before serving.

NUTRITIONAL ANALYSIS PER SERVING: Calories 33 (Kilojoules 139); Protein 0 g; Carbohydrates 9 g; Total Fat 0 g; Saturated Fat 0 g; Cholesterol 0 mg; Sodium 146 mg; Dietary Fiber 0 g

Rice Stick Noodles with Grilled Pork

PREP TIME: 2 HOURS

COOKING TIME: 20 MINUTES,
    PLUS PREPARING FIRE

INGREDIENTS

1 lb (500 g) boneless pork loin

¼ cup (2 oz/60 g) sugar

1 teaspoon lemon juice

½ teaspoon ground pepper

2 shallots, finely minced

2 tablespoons peanut or corn oil

1½ teaspoons each soy sauce and
    fish sauce

FOR THE GARLIC-LIME DIPPING
    SAUCE

¼ cup (2 oz/60 g) sugar

¼ cup (2 fl oz/60 ml) hot water

1 red serrano chile

2 cloves garlic, chopped

⅓ cup (3 fl oz/80 ml) lime juice

¼ cup (2 fl oz/60 ml) fish sauce

1 lb (500 g) dried rice stick noodles

4 tablespoons (⅓ oz/10 g) each
    coarsely chopped fresh mint and
    fresh cilantro (fresh coriander)

1 cup (5 oz/155 g) finely julienned
    peeled cucumber

1 carrot, peeled and finely julienned

1 fresh red serrano chile, seeded
    and finely sliced

1 cup (3 oz/90 g) finely shredded
    red cabbage

¼ cup (1 oz/30 g) coarsely chopped
    roasted peanuts

SERVES 6

❀ Enclose the pork in plastic wrap and place in a freezer until partially frozen, about 1 hour. Meanwhile, in a small, heavy saucepan over medium heat, combine the sugar and ⅓ cup (3 fl oz/80 ml) cold water. Bring to a boil, swirl the pan, and cook just until large, thick, deep brown bubbles form, 5–8 minutes. Do not allow the sugar syrup to burn. Remove from the heat and carefully stir in ¼ cup (2 fl oz/60 ml) hot water. Place over medium-high heat and cook, stirring constantly, until the sugar is caramelized and forms a light syrup that coats the back of a spoon, about 3 minutes longer. Remove from the heat and add the lemon juice and pepper. Pour into a large bowl and let cool. Stir in the shallots, oil, soy sauce, and fish sauce.

❀ Cut the pork across the grain into very thin slices, then into strips 1 inch (2.5 cm) wide. Place between 2 sheets of plastic wrap. Using a meat pounder, gently pound the strips until slightly flattened. Add to the caramelized sugar mixture. Cover and refrigerate for 20 minutes.

❀ To make the sauce, in a bowl, combine the sugar and hot water, stirring to dissolve the sugar. Seed and finely chop the serrano chile. Add to the sauce with the garlic, lime juice, and fish sauce.

❀ Place the rice noodles in a bowl, add warm water to cover, and soak until soft, about 15 minutes. Drain. Bring a large pot three-fourths full of water to a boil; add the noodles and cook until tender, about 1 minute. Drain, rinse with cold running water, and drain again thoroughly.

❀ Prepare a fire in a grill.

❀ Divide 2 tablespoons each of the mint and cilantro among 6 bowls. Drizzle each with 1 tablespoon dipping sauce. Divide the noodles among the bowls and top with equal amounts of the cucumber, carrot, chile, and cabbage and the remaining mint and cilantro. Cover and refrigerate.

❀ Oil the grill rack, lay the pork strips flat directly on the rack, and grill, turning once, until marked with grill lines, about 2 minutes on each side. Divide the pork strips among the bowls, placing them on the noodles. Sprinkle with the peanuts, drizzle with the remaining dipping sauce, and serve at once.

NUTRITIONAL ANALYSIS PER SERVING: Calories 580 (Kilojoules 2,436); Protein 17 g; Carbohydrates 84 g; Total Fat 20 g; Saturated Fat 6 g; Cholesterol 53 mg; Sodium 674 mg; Dietary Fiber 1 g

Dry-Fried Green Beans

PREP TIME: 20 MINUTES

COOKING TIME: 15 MINUTES

INGREDIENTS

4 tablespoons (2 fl oz/60 ml) peanut oil, or more if needed

1 lb (500 g) green beans, trimmed and cut into 2-inch (5-cm) pieces

1 tablespoon dried baby shrimp (prawns)

1½ teaspoons peanut oil

1 tablespoon peeled and finely minced fresh ginger

3 cloves garlic, minced

¼ lb (125 g) ground (minced) pork butt

1 piece Sichuan preserved vegetable, about 1 inch (2.5 cm), rinsed and minced (optional)

1 green (spring) onion, including tender green tops, chopped

1 teaspoon sugar

large pinch of ground white pepper

2 teaspoons soy sauce

2 tablespoons chicken broth

Asian sesame oil to taste

PREP TIP: A "vegetarian" version of this dish may be made without the ground pork.

Chinese dry-fried dishes have sauces that cling like a glaze to the ingredients. During the last seconds of cooking, broth is added to the hot wok and is quickly reduced over high heat, intensifying the flavors and infusing the green beans. Sichuan preserved vegetable (*ja choy*) is actually the knobby stem of a mustard green preserved in salt and chili powder. Used sparingly, it adds crunch and piquant flavor to a dish. Sold in cans, it should be transferred to a jar after opening. Store it, refrigerated, indefinitely.

SERVES 4–6

❀ In a wok over medium-high heat, warm 2 tablespoons of the peanut oil. Add one-third of the green beans and cook, stirring occasionally, until crisp and slightly charred and blistered, about 2 minutes. Transfer to a plate and set aside. Repeat the process twice to cook the remaining beans. If your wok is well seasoned, you will need only 1 tablespoon of oil for each batch.

❀ Place the shrimp in a small bowl, add warm water to cover, and soak for 5 minutes. Drain and mince.

❀ Reheat the wok over medium-high heat and add the 1½ teaspoons peanut oil. Add the ginger and garlic and toss and stir for 15 seconds. Add the pork, shrimp, and preserved vegetable, and toss and stir until the mixture is crumbled and dry, about 2 minutes. Add the green onion, sugar, pepper, and soy sauce; mix thoroughly. Raise the heat to high, return the green beans to the wok, add the chicken broth, and toss vigorously until the liquid is reduced and absorbed, about 2 minutes. Season to taste with sesame oil.

❀ Transfer to a serving dish and serve hot.

NUTRITIONAL ANALYSIS PER SERVING: Calories 208 (Kilojoules 874); Protein 7 g; Carbohydrates 8 g; Total Fat 17 g; Saturated Fat 4 g; Cholesterol 25 mg; Sodium 189 mg; Dietary Fiber 2 g

Braised Noodles with Chicken and Vegetables

PREP TIME: 40 MINUTES

COOKING TIME: 20 MINUTES

INGREDIENTS

3 qt (3 l) water

1½ teaspoons salt

1 lb (500 g) fresh Shanghai-style noodles (see note)

¼ lb (125 g) fresh shiitake mushrooms or 2 oz (60 g) dried shiitake mushrooms

3 tablespoons corn or peanut oil

2 cloves garlic, chopped

½ lb (250 g) skinless, boneless chicken breast, cut into very thin strips about 1½ inches (4 cm) long

1 carrot, peeled and julienned

4 cups (12 oz/375 g) finely shredded both white and red cabbage

2 oz (60 g) garlic chives, cut into 2-inch (5-cm) pieces, or 8 green (spring) onions, cut into 2-inch (5-cm) pieces

¾ cup (6 fl oz/180 ml) chicken broth

3 tablespoons dark soy sauce

2 tablespoons Chinese black rice vinegar or balsamic vinegar

2 teaspoons Asian sesame oil

1 teaspoon oyster sauce

¼ teaspoon sugar

large pinch of ground white pepper

These noodles make a quick dinner on a busy workday. Shanghai noodles are thick, dense wheat-flour noodles that have a chewy texture. You can also use Chinese-style egg noodles; cook them for only 1 minute. Use only 6 tablespoons (3 fl oz/90 ml) of the chicken broth for braising the noodles, which will cook in half the time as Shanghai noodles.

SERVES 4

❀ In a large pot, bring the water and 1 teaspoon of the salt to a boil. Add the noodles, stir well, and cook until just tender, 3–4 minutes. Drain and rinse thoroughly under cold running water. Drain and set aside.

❀ If using fresh shiitakes, remove the stems and discard. If using dried shiitakes, place in a small bowl, cover with warm water, and soak until soft, about 20 minutes. Drain, squeezing out any excess liquid. Remove the stems and discard. Cut the caps into slices ¼ inch (6 mm) thick.

❀ Heat a wok over medium-high heat. Add 2 tablespoons of the oil and the remaining ½ teaspoon salt. Add the garlic and mushrooms and toss and stir until beginning to wilt, about 3 minutes. Add the chicken and toss with the mushrooms until the chicken is opaque, about 3 minutes longer. Transfer to a bowl and set aside.

❀ Raise the heat to high and add the remaining 1 tablespoon oil to the wok. Add the carrot and cabbage and toss and stir until beginning to wilt. Add the garlic chives or green onions and toss and stir for just 10 seconds. Remove from the heat and add to the chicken mixture.

❀ Place the wok over medium-high heat and add the broth, soy sauce, vinegar, sesame oil, oyster sauce, sugar, and pepper. Bring to a boil and cook until the liquid is slightly reduced, about 1 minute. Add the noodles and toss to coat evenly. Cook until the liquid is completely reduced, about 3 minutes. Add the chicken mixture and toss until well combined.

❀ Divide among individual plates and serve immediately.

NUTRITIONAL ANALYSIS PER SERVING: Calories 563 (Kilojoules 2,365); Protein 30 g; Carbohydrates 74 g; Total Fat 17 g; Saturated Fat 2 g; Cholesterol 116 mg; Sodium 1,759 mg; Dietary Fiber 6 g

Stir-Fried Pea Shoots with Garlic

PREP TIME: 10 MINUTES

COOKING TIME: 5 MINUTES

INGREDIENTS

1 lb (500 g) pea shoots

2 tablespoons peanut oil

3 cloves garlic, chopped

1 slice fresh ginger, peeled and
  crushed

½ teaspoon salt

2 tablespoons chicken broth

pinch of sugar

Asian sesame oil to taste

SERVING TIP: Offer this simple side
dish along with main courses such
as grilled chicken or fish.

Pea shoots, the curly tendrils and top pair of leaves of young green pea plants, have a delicate, sweet flavor. The only preparation they require is rinsing in cold water and drying in a salad spinner. Look for pea shoots in an Asian market; if they are unavailable, substitute spinach or watercress.

SERVES 4

❀ Rinse the pea shoots in cold running water. Drain and dry in a salad spinner or thoroughly pat dry with paper towels.

❀ Warm a wok over medium heat. Add the oil, garlic, ginger, and salt and toss and stir until fragrant, about 30 seconds. Raise the heat to high, add 2 or 3 handfuls of pea shoots, and toss and stir until wilted, about 30 seconds. Push the shoots up the sides of the wok and add another 2 or 3 handfuls. Toss and stir until wilted, about 30 seconds. Push the shoots up the sides of the wok and repeat until all the pea shoots have been added to the wok and cooked. If water accumulates in the bottom of the wok, push the shoots up the sides to allow the liquid to reduce. Add the broth and sugar and toss and stir until the liquid is reduced to a few tablespoons, 1–2 minutes. Season with sesame oil.

❀ Transfer to a bowl and serve immediately.

NUTRITIONAL ANALYSIS PER SERVING: Calories 211 (Kilojoules 886); Protein 10 g; Carbohydrates 33 g; Total Fat 8 g; Saturated Fat 1 g; Cholesterol 0 mg; Sodium 344 mg; Dietary Fiber 0 g

Striped Bass Grilled in Banana Leaves

PREP TIME: 1½ HOURS

COOKING TIME: 20 MINUTES,
    PLUS PREPARING FIRE

INGREDIENTS

FOR THE SPICE PASTE
6 large cloves garlic, halved

1 piece fresh ginger, 1 inch (2.5 cm),
    peeled

3 tablespoons fresh cilantro (fresh
    coriander) roots or stems

¾ teaspoon each salt and whole
    peppercorns, cracked

1½ tablespoons Chinese light
    soy sauce

2 whole striped bass, sea bass, red
    snapper, or trout, about 1½ lb
    (750 g) each, heads and tails intact

salt and ground pepper to taste

2 stalks lemongrass, trimmed, crushed,
    and cut into 2-inch (5-cm) lengths

2 large banana leaves, or more if
    needed

1 tablespoon vegetable oil, or as
    needed

FOR THE GARLIC-LIME SAUCE
4 green serrano chiles, chopped

3 cloves garlic, chopped

1 shallot, chopped

⅓ cup (3 fl oz/80 ml) chicken broth

1 tablespoon sugar

¼ teaspoon salt

juice of 2 limes

2 tablespoons chopped fresh
    cilantro (fresh coriander)

For this Thai dish, you need banana leaves that are 6 inches (15 cm) longer and three times wider than each fish.

SERVES 4

✸ To make the spice paste, in a mortar or in a blender, combine the garlic, ginger, cilantro roots or stems, salt, and peppercorns. Grind with a pestle or blend until a smooth paste forms. Stir in the soy sauce. Set aside.

✸ Rinse the fish under cold running water and pat dry with paper towels. Make 3 diagonal slashes, about 2 inches (5 cm) apart, almost to the bone across both sides of each fish. Sprinkle inside and out with salt and pepper. Stuff the cavities with the lemongrass, dividing evenly, and rub the spice paste inside both fish.

✸ Bring a pot three-fourths full of water to a boil. Dip each banana leaf into the water until softened, about 4 seconds. Wipe dry. Set the leaves, glossy sides down, on a work surface and brush the centers with the oil. Place 1 fish in the center of each banana leaf. Fold the long sides up and over the fish so they overlap in the middle and secure with toothpicks. Fold the ends over to enclose the sides and thread toothpicks into the leaves to make a neat packet. If the leaves tear, wrap with extra leaves.

✸ Prepare a fire in a grill.

✸ Meanwhile, prepare the garlic-lime sauce: In a saucepan over medium-high heat, combine the chiles, garlic, shallot, broth, sugar, and salt and bring to a boil. Reduce the heat to low, stir to combine, and simmer, uncovered, until reduced to a light syrup, about 3 minutes. Let cool and mix in the lime juice and cilantro. Transfer to a bowl.

✸ When the coals are hot, place the fish packets on the grill rack and grill, turning every 3–4 minutes. The total cooking time is about 15 minutes. The fish should sizzle constantly while cooking. To check for doneness, carefully remove a fish packet from the grill. Using scissors, snip the banana leaf lengthwise along the center to open the packet. The fish should be opaque; if not, rewrap and continue cooking.

✸ Serve hot with the garlic-lime sauce.

NUTRITIONAL ANALYSIS PER SERVING: Calories 204 (Kilojoules 857); Protein 25 g; Carbohydrates 10 g; Total Fat 7 g; Saturated Fat 1 g; Cholesterol 106 mg; Sodium 1,142 mg; Dietary Fiber 1 g

Chicken and Asparagus with Spicy Black Bean Sauce

PREP TIME: 40 MINUTES

COOKING TIME: 10 MINUTES

INGREDIENTS

1½ tablespoons peanut oil

2 cloves garlic, chopped

2 tablespoons Chinese preserved black beans, rinsed with cold water and drained

1 teaspoon peeled and chopped fresh ginger

½ teaspoon salt

¾ lb (375 g) asparagus, trimmed and cut on the diagonal into 1½-inch (4-cm) pieces

½ yellow onion, thinly sliced

½ red bell pepper (capsicum), cut into ½-inch (12-mm) cubes

¾ lb (375 g) boneless, skinless chicken thighs, cut into ½-inch (12-mm) cubes

¾ cup (6 fl oz/180 ml) chicken broth

1 tablespoon soy sauce

½ teaspoon sugar

1 large red jalapeño chile, seeded and chopped

1½ tablespoons cornstarch (corn flour) mixed with 2 tablespoons water

1 teaspoon oyster sauce (optional)

1 teaspoon Asian sesame oil

This stir-fry is especially delicious poured over a plate of hot steaming rice. Chinese preserved black beans are salted fermented black soybeans. When stir-fried, they exude a pungent and rich savory flavor. Use asparagus that is not too thin and not too fat.

SERVES 4

❋ Heat a wok over medium-high heat. Add the oil, garlic, black beans, ginger, and salt and toss and stir until fragrant, about 1 minute. Raise the heat to high, add the asparagus, onion, and bell pepper, and toss and stir until coated with oil and seared, about 1 minute.

❋ Add the chicken and toss and stir until opaque and firm, about 2 minutes. Add the broth, soy sauce, sugar, and chile, bring to a boil, cover, and cook until the asparagus is tender but still crunchy, about 1 minute longer. Add the cornstarch mixture and the oyster sauce, if using, and cook, stirring continuously, until the sauce thickens, about 30 seconds.

❋ Stir in the sesame oil and serve hot.

NUTRITIONAL ANALYSIS PER SERVING: Calories 223 (Kilojoules 937); Protein 20 g; Carbohydrates 13 g; Total Fat 10 g; Saturated Fat 2 g; Cholesterol 71 mg; Sodium 1,032 mg; Dietary Fiber 2 g

Tandoori Chicken and Toasted Pappadams

PREP TIME: 20 MINUTES, PLUS
4½ HOURS FOR MARINATING

COOKING TIME: 45 MINUTES

INGREDIENTS

3 lb (1.5 kg) skinless chicken thighs or breasts, or a combination

3 tablespoons lime or lemon juice

FOR THE MARINADE

1 tablespoon coriander seeds

1 teaspoon cumin seeds

4 cloves garlic

1 piece fresh ginger, about 1 inch (2.5 cm), peeled

1 teaspoon salt

1–2 tablespoons water

1 teaspoon paprika

½ teaspoon ground turmeric

½ teaspoon cayenne pepper

½ cup (4 oz/125 g) plain yogurt

1 tablespoon lime juice

8 pappadam wafers

3 tablespoons ghee or vegetable oil

1 white onion, thinly sliced

1 small English (hothouse) cucumber, peeled and thinly sliced

3 tablespoons coarsely chopped fresh cilantro (fresh coriander)

2 tablespoons coarsely chopped fresh mint

2 limes, cut lengthwise into wedges

The marinade of yogurt and lime juice tenderizes and moistens the meat. Pappadams, flatbreads made from lentil flour, typically accompany Indian meals. Serve basmati rice alongside.

SERVES 6–8

❀ Pat the chicken pieces dry with paper towels. Make deep diagonal slashes almost to the bone at 1½-inch (4-cm) intervals across the meaty side of each piece. Place in a glass bowl and rub on both sides with the lime or lemon juice. Cover and refrigerate for 30 minutes.

❀ Meanwhile, prepare the marinade: In a small, dry frying pan over low heat, toast the coriander and cumin seeds, stirring occasionally, until fragrant, about 3 minutes. Transfer to a spice grinder and grind to a powder, or transfer to a mortar and grind to a powder with a pestle. In a blender, combine the garlic, ginger, salt, and enough water to facilitate blending. Process until a smooth paste forms. Add the cumin and coriander seeds, paprika, turmeric, cayenne, yogurt, and lime juice and purée until smooth. Pour into a large lock-top plastic bag, add the chicken pieces, seal, and turn the bag to coat the pieces evenly. Refrigerate for at least 4 hours or as long as overnight.

❀ Preheat a broiler (griller). Bring the chicken to room temperature.

❀ If using the pappadams, place a cake rack over a gas or electric burner. Working with 1 pappadam at a time, place on the rack over medium-high heat. Using tongs, rotate continuously until completely opaque and covered with tiny bubbles and brown flecks, about 30 seconds. Turn and toast on the second side until crisp, about 30 seconds longer.

❀ Place the chicken, slashed sides up, on a broiler pan and brush with the ghee or oil. Broil (grill) 2–3 inches (5–7.5 cm) from the heat source until browned, about 20 minutes. Turn, brush with ghee or oil, and grill until browned on the second side, about 10 minutes longer.

❀ Transfer to a serving platter and top evenly with the onion and cucumber slices. Sprinkle with the cilantro and mint, garnish with the lime wedges, and serve with the pappadams.

NUTRITIONAL ANALYSIS PER SERVING: Calories 248 (Kilojoules 1,042); Protein 30 g; Carbohydrates 8 g; Total Fat 10 g; Saturated Fat 2 g; Cholesterol 98 mg; Sodium 452 mg; Dietary Fiber 1 g

Curried Potatoes, Cauliflower, and Peas

PREP TIME: 30 MINUTES

COOKING TIME: 20 MINUTES

INGREDIENTS

1½ lb (750 g) red new or Yukon gold potatoes

2 teaspoons brown mustard seeds

2 tablespoons ghee or vegetable oil

1 yellow onion, sliced

2 cloves garlic, finely minced

2 teaspoons peeled and finely minced fresh ginger

1 teaspoon ground cumin

1 teaspoon garam masala

½ teaspoon ground turmeric

¼ teaspoon cayenne pepper

2 cups (4 oz/125 g) small cauliflower florets

1 cup (8 fl oz/250 ml) water

salt and ground black pepper to taste

1 cup (5 oz/155 g) fresh or thawed frozen petite peas

2 tablespoons chopped fresh cilantro (fresh coriander)

Brown mustard seeds are found in Indian markets and specialty-food stores. As they are being toasted or fried, they pop and sputter in the pan. Toasting the seeds releases their nutty flavor. This pungent and savory vegetable stew is delicious served as a vegetarian main course or with roasted or grilled meats.

SERVES 6

❀ Peel the potatoes and cut into 1-inch (2.5-cm) cubes. Place in a bowl, add water to cover, and set aside.

❀ In a large saucepan over medium heat, add the mustard seeds and cook until they begin to pop, 1–2 minutes. Add the ghee or oil, onion, garlic, and ginger and cook, stirring occasionally, until the onion begins to soften, about 1 minute. Sprinkle in the cumin, garam masala, turmeric, and cayenne and cook, stirring constantly, until fragrant, about 30 seconds. Drain the potatoes. Add the potatoes and cauliflower and stir to coat with the spices. Add the water, cover, and cook until the potatoes are almost tender, 10–12 minutes. Season with salt and pepper. Add the peas and cook until tender and the liquid is absorbed, about 3 minutes longer.

❀ Garnish with the cilantro and serve hot or at room temperature.

NUTRITIONAL ANALYSIS PER SERVING: Calories 163 (Kilojoules 685); Protein 4 g; Carbohydrates 26 g; Total Fat 5 g; Saturated Fat 1 g; Cholesterol 0 mg; Sodium 42 mg; Dietary Fiber 4 g

Scallops, Eggplant, and Squash in Green Curry Sauce

PREP TIME: 25 MINUTES

COOKING TIME: 25 MINUTES

INGREDIENTS

1 can (13½ fl oz/425 ml) unsweetened coconut milk

2 tablespoons prepared Thai green
curry paste

1 tablespoon fish sauce

1 teaspoon palm sugar or dark
brown sugar, or to taste

8 fresh or frozen kaffir lime leaves,
plus 3 leaves, finely slivered, for
garnish

1 yellow summer squash, cut into
irregular ¾-inch (2-cm) chunks

1 small zucchini (courgette), cut into
irregular ¾-inch (2-cm) chunks

2 teaspoons vegetable oil

1 lb (500 g) large sea scallops

salt and ground pepper to taste

2 Asian (slender) eggplants
(aubergines), cut into irregular
¾-inch (2-cm) chunks

½ cup (½ oz/15 g) Thai basil leaves
or sweet basil

For this Thai curry, scallops are seared and immersed in a creamy sauce. Serve this hearty curry with steamed rice and a vegetable dish such as Stir-Fried Pea Shoots with Garlic (page 66) or Spicy Asparagus Bean Salad (page 43).

SERVES 4

❀ Open the can of coconut milk without shaking it and spoon ⅓ cup (3 fl oz/80 ml) of the cream at the top into a wide saucepan. Place over medium-high heat; add the green curry paste and cook, stirring fre-quently, until beads of oil appear in the paste, about 5 minutes. Add the fish sauce, sugar, 8 lime leaves, and remaining coconut milk and cook, uncovered, stirring constantly, until the mixture is the consistency of a cream sauce, about 5 minutes. Set aside.

❀ Bring a saucepan three-fourths full of water to a boil. Add the squash and zucchini and blanch until tender-crisp, 2–3 minutes. Drain and rinse under cold running water to halt the cooking.

❀ Warm a wide, heavy frying pan over medium-high heat. Add ½ tea-spoon of the oil and tilt the pan to spread the oil evenly over the bottom. Remove any excess oil with paper towels. When the oil is nearly smok-ing, place the scallops, in one layer, in the pan and cook, turning once, until seared, about 1 minute on each side. Season with salt and pepper, transfer to a plate, cover loosely, and keep warm. Return the pan to medium-high heat and warm the remaining 1½ teaspoons of the oil. Add the eggplant cubes and cook, stirring constantly, until they begin to soften and are well browned at the edges, 3–5 minutes. Add the squash and zucchini, the sauce, and the basil and cook until the basil wilts and the sauce is heated through, about 30 seconds. Add the scallops and stir gently to coat with the sauce.

❀ Serve hot, garnished with the slivered lime leaves.

NUTRITIONAL ANALYSIS PER SERVING: Calories 362 (Kilojoules 1,520); Protein 23 g; Carbohydrates 15 g; Total Fat 24 g; Saturated Fat 19 g; Cholesterol 38 mg; Sodium 731 mg; Dietary Fiber 2 g

Soft-Shell Crabs with Chile Sauce

PREP TIME: 1 HOUR

COOKING TIME: 15 MINUTES

INGREDIENTS

FOR THE CHILE SAUCE

4 cloves garlic

4 red jalapeño chiles, seeded

1 piece fresh ginger, about
    1½ inches (4 cm), peeled

2–4 tablespoons water

2 tablespoons peanut or corn oil

¼ cup (2 fl oz/60 ml) tomato paste
    or tomato ketchup

1 tablespoon Sriracha sauce or
    sweet chile sauce

1 tablespoon soy sauce

1 tablespoon brown sugar

1 cup (8 fl oz/250 ml) chicken broth

1 tablespoon cornstarch (cornflour)
    mixed with 3 tablespoons water

1 tablespoon lime juice or red wine
    vinegar

1 extra-large egg

6 soft-shell crabs, about 4 oz (125 g)
    each

¼ cup (1 oz/30 g) cornstarch
    (cornflour)

3 tablespoons peanut or corn oil

salt and ground pepper to taste

2 green (spring) onions, including
    tender green tops, chopped,
    for garnish

6 sprigs fresh cilantro (fresh
    coriander), for garnish

In this signature Singaporean dish, soft-shell crabs are sautéed, then bathed in a rich, sweet, tangy sauce. To speed preparation, ask the fishmonger to clean the crabs. Accompany with steamed rice or chunks of French bread to sop up the sauce.

SERVES 2

⊛ To make the sauce, in a blender, combine the garlic, chiles, ginger, and just enough water to facilitate blending. Process until a smooth paste forms.

⊛ Warm a wok over medium heat. Add the oil, stir in the paste mixture, and cook until fragrant and creamy, about 1 minute. Stir in the tomato paste or ketchup, Sriracha or chile sauce, soy sauce, sugar, and broth. Add the cornstarch mixture and cook, stirring constantly, until the sauce thickens, about 30 seconds. Add the lime juice or vinegar. Crack the egg into the wok and cook, without stirring, until it begins to set, about 2 minutes. Fold the egg into the sauce; do not overmix. Specks of egg should peek through the sauce. Remove from the heat, cover, and keep warm.

⊛ Place each crab on its back and twist or cut off the small, triangular apron-shaped shell flap. Turn the crab, lift up the shell, and, using your fingers or kitchen scissors, remove and discard any gray gills. Using scissors, cut off the eyes and mouth. Scoop out the soft matter just inside this cut and discard. Rinse the crab and pat dry with paper towels.

⊛ Dust the crabs with the cornstarch, shaking off any excess. In a large frying pan over medium-high heat, warm the oil. Add the crabs and fry, turning once, until brown and crisp, about 3 minutes on each side. Season with salt and pepper.

⊛ Add the crabs to the chile sauce and turn to coat evenly. Garnish with the green onions and cilantro and serve.

NUTRITIONAL ANALYSIS PER SERVING: Calories 704 (Kilojoules 2,957); Protein 40 g; Carbohydrates 40 g; Total Fat 50 g; Saturated Fat 9 g; Cholesterol 417 mg; Sodium 2,657 mg; Dietary Fiber 3 g

Beef Braised in Star Anise Sauce

PREP TIME: 1 HOUR

COOKING TIME: 1¾ HOURS

INGREDIENTS

2½ lb (1.25 kg) boneless beef chuck, cut into irregular 1½-inch (4-cm) chunks

1 tablespoon dark soy sauce

1 tablespoon cornstarch (cornflour)

1 teaspoon granulated sugar

2 tablespoons peanut or corn oil

4 green (spring) onions, including green tops, cut into 2-inch (5-cm) pieces

4 cloves garlic, crushed

2 pieces fresh ginger, 1 inch (2.5 cm) each, peeled and crushed

1 teaspoon salt

¼ cup (2 fl oz/60 ml) Chinese rice wine or dry sherry

¼ cup (2 fl oz/60 ml) dark soy sauce

1 piece rock sugar, about 2 inches (5 cm), or 2 tablespoons granulated sugar

6 whole star anise pods

3 cups (24 fl oz/750 ml) boiling water

2 carrots, peeled and cut into irregular 1-inch (2.5-cm) chunks

1½ lb (750 g) daikon or turnips, peeled and cut into irregular 1-inch (2.5-cm) chunks

1½ tablespoons cornstarch (cornflour) mixed with 3 tablespoons water

1 teaspoon Asian sesame oil

This "red-braised" stew is a popular Chinese home-style dish. "Red" refers to the reddish brown color, acquired from the use of dark soy sauce, and distinguishes this dish from "white-braised" dishes, which are cooked in a clear liquid without soy sauce. Serve with steamed rice or boiled Chinese noodles and Stir-Fried Pea Shoots with Garlic (page 66).

SERVES 6

❈ In a large bowl, combine the beef with the 1 tablespoon soy sauce, 1 tablespoon cornstarch, and 1 teaspoon sugar. Toss to coat the beef evenly.

❈ In a dutch oven over medium-high heat, warm the oil. Add the green onions, garlic, ginger, and salt and sauté until aromatic, about 30 seconds. Add the beef in small batches and sauté until browned, about 10 minutes each. Add the rice wine or sherry, ¼ cup (2 fl oz/60 ml) soy sauce, rock or granulated sugar, star anise, and enough of the boiling water to cover the meat. Bring to a boil, cover, reduce the heat to low, and simmer for about 1 hour.

❈ Add the carrots and daikon or turnips and simmer until the beef and vegetables are tender, about 30 minutes longer. Remove the garlic cloves and ginger pieces and discard. Add the cornstarch mixture and cook, stirring occasionally, until the sauce thickens, about 30 seconds.

❈ Stir in the sesame oil and serve hot.

NUTRITIONAL ANALYSIS PER SERVING: Calories 619 (Kilojoules 2,601); Protein 34 g; Carbohydrates 19 g; Total Fat 44 g; Saturated Fat 16 g; Cholesterol 136 mg; Sodium 1,645 mg; Dietary Fiber 1 g

Shrimp and Tomatoes in Chile Sauce

PREP TIME: 20 MINUTES

COOKING TIME: 15 MINUTES

INGREDIENTS

2 candlenuts or blanched almonds

3 shallots, quartered

2 large jalapeño chiles, seeded and quartered

2 cloves garlic, halved

1 teaspoon shrimp paste or anchovy paste

2 tablespoons water, or as needed

3 tablespoons vegetable oil

1 yellow onion, cut into wedges ¾ inch (2 cm) wide

¾ lb (375 g) large shrimp (prawns), peeled and deveined with tails intact, patted dry

1 stalk lemongrass, bruised and cut into 1-inch (2.5-cm) pieces

1 tablespoon sugar

½ teaspoon salt

2 firm tomatoes, cut into wedges ½ inch (12 mm) wide

2–3 tablespoons lime juice

In Malaysia, this dish is called *udang* ("shrimp") *goreng* ("fried"). Cooking the dish is as simple as its translation, but the final result has a complex layering of flavor: a refreshing citrus base accentuated with strong savory notes and a pleasant jolt of spicy heat. Serve with Vegetable Stir-Fry with Bean Thread Noodles (page 44) and steamed rice.

SERVES 4–6

❋ Place the candlenuts or almonds in a small bowl, cover with water, and let stand until moist, about 5 minutes. Drain. In a blender, combine the nuts, shallots, chiles, garlic, shrimp or anchovy paste, and enough water to facilitate blending. Process until a smooth paste forms. Set aside.

❋ Warm a wok over medium-high heat. Add 1 tablespoon of the oil. When hot, add the onion and toss and stir until translucent, about 1 minute. Raise the heat to high, add the shrimp, and toss and stir until they turn bright orange, about 2 minutes. Transfer to a plate.

❋ Return the wok to medium-high heat and add the remaining 2 tablespoons oil. When hot, add the reserved spice paste and the lemongrass and toss and stir until fragrant and blended with the oil, 3–4 minutes. Continue to cook, stirring frequently, until the oil separates from the spice paste, 5–8 minutes. Add the sugar and salt, raise the heat to high, and add the shrimp mixture and the tomatoes. Toss and stir until heated through, about 30 seconds.

❋ Drizzle with the lime juice and serve hot.

NUTRITIONAL ANALYSIS PER SERVING: Calories 180 (Kilojoules 756); Protein 13 g; Carbohydrates 11 g; Total Fat 10 g; Saturated Fat 1 g; Cholesterol 85 mg; Sodium 378 mg; Dietary Fiber 1 g

Kettle-Seared Garlic-Pepper Mussels

PREP TIME: 30 MINUTES

COOKING TIME: 10 MINUTES

INGREDIENTS

2 tablespoons vegetable oil

6 large cloves garlic, chopped

2 large shallots, thinly sliced

½ teaspoon coarse sea salt or
   kosher salt

2–2½ lb (1–1.25 kg) mussels,
   scrubbed and debearded

2 tablespoons sugar

2 tablespoons fish sauce

1 teaspoon coarse-ground pepper

1 red jalapeño chile, seeded and
   finely diced

fresh cilantro (fresh coriander) sprigs,
   for garnish

This quick-cooking Vietnamese-style dish infuses fresh mussels with the intense flavors of garlic, pepper, and fish sauce. It is best made in a cast-iron kettle. Cast-iron pans get very hot, enabling the mussels to cook quickly and heightening the flavors of the seasonings. If you don't have a kettle, use a wok or dutch oven.

SERVES 4

❈ Warm a 3-qt (3-l) cast-iron kettle or wok over medium-high heat. Add the oil, garlic, shallots, and salt and sauté until the garlic and shallots are golden brown, about 1 minute. Raise the heat to high and add the mussels, discarding any that do not close to the touch. Toss and stir to coat with the seasoned oil. Add the sugar, fish sauce, and pepper and stir to combine. Reduce the heat to medium-high, cover, and cook until the mussels open, 3–5 minutes. Discard any mussels that did not open. The sauce should be the consistency of a light syrup. If the sauce is too thin, using a slotted spoon, transfer the mussels to a plate. Raise the heat to high and cook the sauce, stirring frequently, until reduced, 3–5 minutes. Return the mussels to the kettle or wok and toss to coat with the sauce.

❈ Garnish with the chile and cilantro sprigs and serve hot.

NUTRITIONAL ANALYSIS PER SERVING: Calories 183 (Kilojoules 769); Protein 11 g; Carbohydrates 14 g; Total Fat 9 g; Saturated Fat 1 g; Cholesterol 21 mg; Sodium 694 mg; Dietary Fiber 0 g

Spicy Grilled Chicken with Kaffir Lime

PREP TIME: 1 HOUR, PLUS
   1 HOUR FOR MARINATING

COOKING TIME: 45 MINUTES

INGREDIENTS

3 small chickens, about 2 lb (1 kg)
   each, quartered

1 tablespoon lime juice

3 teaspoons salt

4 candlenuts or blanched almonds

8 red jalapeño chiles, seeded and
   quartered

6 cloves garlic, sliced

5 stalks lemongrass, center white
   part only, chopped

5 shallots or 1 small yellow onion,
   quartered

1 piece fresh ginger, about ¾ inch
   (2 cm)

1 teaspoon ground turmeric

2–4 tablespoons water

1 can (13½ fl oz/425 ml) unsweetened coconut milk, shaken well

¼ cup (2 fl oz/60 ml) peanut or
   corn oil

2 tablespoons sugar

10 fresh or frozen kaffir lime leaves,
   center spines removed and very
   finely shredded

2 limes, cut lengthwise into wedges

6 sprigs fresh cilantro (fresh coriander)

Fragrant and flavorful lemongrass and kaffir lime permeate this Indonesian-style grilled chicken. Much of the preparation can be done in advance, making the chicken ideal for outdoor cooking.

SERVES 6

❀ Using a fork, pierce the chicken quarters all over. Place in a glass bowl, rub with the lime juice and 1 teaspoon of the salt, and set aside.

❀ Place the candlenuts or almonds in a small bowl, add water to cover, and soak until moist, about 10 minutes. Drain. In a blender, combine the nuts, jalapeños, garlic, lemongrass, shallots or onion, ginger, turmeric, and just enough of the water to facilitate blending. Process until a smooth paste forms. Transfer to a large bowl and add the coconut milk. You should have about 3 cups (24 fl oz/750 ml). Add ½ cup (4 fl oz/125 ml) to the chicken, coat evenly, cover, and refrigerate for at least 1 hour or up to overnight. Refrigerate the remaining liquid.

❀ Warm a wok over medium heat. Add the oil and the remaining coconut milk mixture and cook, stirring frequently, until emulsified and fragrant, about 3 minutes. Continue to cook, stirring occasionally, until beads of oil appear in the mixture, about 8 minutes. Add the sugar, remaining 2 teaspoons salt, and three-fourths of the shredded lime leaves, reduce the heat to low, and simmer until the sugar is dissolved, about 1 minute. Taste and adjust the seasonings. Set the sauce aside.

❀ Prepare a fire in a grill.

❀ When the coals are hot, place the chicken, skin side down, directly on the grill rack and grill until golden brown, about 15 minutes. Using tongs, turn and cook until golden brown, about 15 minutes. An instant-read thermometer inserted into the thickest part of the breast away from the bone should register 170°F (77°C) and in the thigh should register 185°F (85°C). Transfer the chicken to a serving dish.

❀ Reheat the sauce over medium heat and pour over the chicken. Garnish with the remaining lime shreds, the lime wedges, and the cilantro and serve.

NUTRITIONAL ANALYSIS PER SERVING: Calories 734 (Kilojoules 3,083); Protein 57 g; Carbohydrates 14 g; Total Fat 50 g; Saturated Fat 21 g; Cholesterol 176 mg; Sodium 1,342 mg; Dietary Fiber 1 g

Grilled Chicken, Korean Style

PREP TIME: 40 MINUTES, PLUS
3 HOURS FOR MARINATING

COOKING TIME: 15 MINUTES,
PLUS PREPARING FIRE

INGREDIENTS

1½ lb (750 g) skinless, boneless
chicken breasts, thighs, or a
combination

2 tablespoons lemon juice

2 tablespoons sesame seeds

2 cloves garlic, minced

2 green (spring) onions, including
tender green tops, minced, plus
3 green onions, white parts only,
cut into fine slivers

¼ cup (2 fl oz/60 ml) light soy sauce

¼ cup (2 fl oz/60 ml) dark soy sauce

2 tablespoons sugar

1½ tablespoons Asian sesame oil

2 teaspoons peeled and minced
fresh ginger

½ teaspoon ground pepper

COOKING TIP: The chicken can also
be cooked on the stove top. Preheat a
flat cast-iron grill pan over medium-
high heat until water sprinkled in
the pan immediately forms beads
that dance across the surface. Add
1–2 teaspoons vegetable oil and
spread across the surface with several
layers of paper towels, wiping off any
excess oil. Place the chicken pieces
in one layer. Cook, turning once, until
charred, about 6 minutes on each side.

Seasonings typical of Korean cooking—soy sauce, garlic, ginger, toasted sesame seeds, and green onions—flavor this grilled chicken, called *dak bulgogi*. Serve with steamed rice and stir-fried spinach or other leafy greens.

SERVES 6

❀ Place each chicken piece between 2 sheets of plastic wrap. Using a meat pounder, gently pound until a uniform thickness of ¼ inch (6 mm). Place in a glass bowl and rub evenly with the lemon juice.

❀ In a small, dry frying pan over low heat, toast the sesame seeds, stirring occasionally, until fragrant and golden brown, 3–5 minutes. Set aside 1 tablespoon of the toasted seeds. Transfer the remaining 1 tablespoon seeds to a spice grinder and grind to a powder, or transfer to a mortar and grind with a pestle.

❀ In a small bowl, stir together the ground sesame seeds, garlic, minced green onions, soy sauces, sugar, sesame oil, ginger, and pepper. Pour over the chicken, turn the pieces to coat evenly, cover, and refrigerate for at least 3 hours or as long as overnight.

❀ Prepare a fire in a grill.

❀ When the coals are hot, place the chicken pieces directly on the grill rack. Grill until lightly charred, about 5 minutes. Turn and cook until charred on the second side, 3–4 minutes longer. Transfer to a serving platter.

❀ Sprinkle with the reserved sesame seeds and the slivered green onions and serve.

NUTRITIONAL ANALYSIS PER SERVING: Calories 223 (Kilojoules 937); Protein 24 g; Carbohydrates 10 g; Total Fat 9 g; Saturated Fat 2 g; Cholesterol 94 mg; Sodium 1,666 mg; Dietary Fiber 1 g

Grilled Duck with Red Curry Sauce

PREP TIME: 45 MINUTES, PLUS
4 HOURS FOR MARINATING

COOKING TIME: 25 MINUTES,
PLUS PREPARING FIRE

INGREDIENTS

1 clove garlic, minced

1 tablespoon granulated sugar

1 tablespoon rice wine or dry sherry

2 teaspoons light soy sauce

1½ teaspoons Asian sesame oil

1 teaspoon dark soy sauce

1 teaspoon peeled and minced fresh
    ginger

½ teaspoon five-spice powder

½ teaspoon salt, plus salt to taste

6 duck breast halves, about 4–6 oz
    (125–185 g) each

2 cans (13½ fl oz/425 ml each)
    unsweetened coconut milk

2–3 tablespoons Thai red curry paste

1–2 tablespoons Thai fish sauce

1 tablespoon palm sugar or dark
    brown sugar

8 fresh or frozen kaffir lime leaves

4 red chiles, seeded and sliced

1 cup (6 oz/185 g) diced fresh
    pineapple

½ cup (½ oz/15 g) fresh Thai basil or
    sweet basil, plus leaves for garnish

ground pepper to taste

Roasted Chinese duck—as seen hanging in storefront windows—
is traditionally used for this Thai recipe. When roasted duck is
not available, you'll find that it is easy to marinate and grill your
own, as directed in the recipe below. Steamed rice makes a
good accompaniment.

SERVES 6

✻ In a large glass bowl, combine the garlic, granulated sugar, rice wine
or sherry, light soy sauce, sesame oil, dark soy sauce, ginger, five-spice
powder, and ½ teaspoon salt. Using a fork, prick the duck skin at 1-inch
(2.5-cm) intervals. Add the duck to the bowl and turn to coat evenly, rub-
bing the marinade on both sides of the breast halves. Cover and refrigerate
for 4 hours or up to overnight.

✻ Prepare a fire in a charcoal grill.

✻ Meanwhile, open the cans of coconut milk without shaking them.
Spoon the thick layer of cream on top into a bowl. In a wok over medium-
high heat, combine ½ cup (4 fl oz/125 ml) of the cream and the red curry
paste and cook, stirring frequently, until the cream is aromatic and
beads of oil float on top, about 3 minutes. Add the fish sauce, sugar,
lime leaves, chiles, and remaining coconut cream and milk. Cook, stirring occasionally, until heated through, about 5 minutes. Stir in the
pineapple and ½ cup (½ oz/15 g) basil. Remove from the heat and keep
warm while grilling the duck.

✻ When the coals are medium-hot, remove the duck from the marinade,
discarding the marinade, and place directly on the grill rack, skin side
down. Grill until the fat is rendered from the skin and the skin is crisp,
about 8 minutes. Turn and grill until the duck is fully cooked and, when
pressed, feels firm to the touch on the second side, 3–5 minutes. Season
with salt and pepper. Cut the duck across the grain into slices ¼ inch
(6 mm) thick.

✻ To serve, arrange 1 sliced duck breast half on each plate. Spoon the
curry sauce over the top and garnish with the basil leaves.

NUTRITIONAL ANALYSIS PER SERVING: Calories 496 (Kilojoules 2,083); Protein 23 g;
Carbohydrates 14 g; Total Fat 40 g; Saturated Fat 27 g; Cholesterol 105 mg; Sodium 702 mg;
Dietary Fiber 1 g

Caramelized Shrimp with Sour Bean Sprouts

PREP TIME: 10 MINUTES, PLUS
1 HOUR FOR STANDING

COOKING TIME: 20 MINUTES

INGREDIENTS

FOR THE BEAN SPROUTS

4 cups (32 fl oz/1 l) water

½ cup (4 fl oz/125 ml) white vinegar

2 tablespoons granulated sugar

1 tablespoon salt

1 lb (500 g) mung bean sprouts

1 carrot, peeled and finely julienned

⅓ cup (2½ oz/75 g) brown sugar

½ cup (4 fl oz/125 ml) water

1 teaspoon lemon juice

1 lb (500 g) large shrimp (prawns),
    peeled, deveined, and patted dry

2 tablespoons fish sauce

2 teaspoons granulated sugar

1 teaspoon peeled and finely minced
    fresh ginger

¼ teaspoon ground pepper

1½ tablespoons peanut or corn oil

3 cloves garlic, minced

3 large shallots, sliced

2 green (spring) onions, including
    tender green tops, cut into 2-inch
    (5-cm) pieces

1 tablespoon lime juice

COOKING TIP: You can use the leftover caramel sauce for stir-frying
meats, poultry, or seafood.

In Vietnam, caramel sauce is primarily used to enrich savory dishes rather than desserts. Sour bean sprouts, a perfect union of sweet, salty, and tart flavors, are the traditional accompaniment and ideal match for caramelized dishes.

SERVES 6

❀ To make the bean sprouts, in a saucepan over high heat, combine the water, vinegar, granulated sugar, and salt and bring to a boil. Let cool. Place the bean sprouts and carrot in a large glass bowl, pour in the vinegar mixture, cover, and let stand at room temperature for 1 hour. Drain and set aside.

❀ In a small, heavy saucepan over high heat, combine the brown sugar and ¼ cup (2 fl oz/60 ml) of the water and bring to a boil. Cook, maintaining a steady boil, until the mixture forms small, sluggish, rich brown bubbles, 5–8 minutes. Immediately remove from the heat and stir in the remaining ¼ cup (2 fl oz/60 ml) water. Bring to a gentle boil over medium-high heat and cook until the caramel is completely dissolved, about 5 minutes longer. Add the lemon juice and set aside. You should have about ⅓ cup (3 fl oz/80 ml) caramel sauce. Extra sauce will keep indefinitely in the refrigerator.

❀ In a bowl, toss the shrimp with the fish sauce, granulated sugar, ginger, and pepper. In a wok or small saucepan over medium heat, warm the oil. Add the garlic and shallots and sauté until golden, about 1 minute. Remove the shrimp from the marinade, reserving the marinade. Raise the heat to medium-high, add the shrimp, and cook until bright pink, about 2 minutes. Add the green onions, the reserved marinade, and 2 tablespoons of the caramel sauce and stir the shrimp to coat evenly. Add the lime juice.

❀ Serve hot with the bean sprouts.

NUTRITIONAL ANALYSIS PER SERVING: Calories 171 (Kilojoules 718); Protein 16 g; Carbohydrates 16 g; Total Fat 5 g; Saturated Fat 1 g; Cholesterol 93 mg; Sodium 593 mg; Dietary Fiber 1 g

Dry Beef Curry

PREP TIME: 1½ HOURS

COOKING TIME: 1¾ HOURS

INGREDIENTS

10–15 dried red chiles, seeded

5 candlenuts or blanched almonds

6 shallots, chopped

4 cloves garlic, chopped

3 slices fresh galangal, chopped, or 1½ slices dried galangal, soaked in water for 20 minutes and chopped

3 stalks lemongrass, center white part only, chopped

4 slices peeled fresh ginger, chopped

1 teaspoon Malaysian dried shrimp paste or anchovy paste

1½ teaspoons each ground coriander and ground cumin

½ teaspoon turmeric

¼ teaspoon each ground fennel and ground cloves

2–4 tablespoons water, or as needed

¼ cup (1 oz/30 g) shredded, dried unsweetened coconut

2 tablespoons vegetable oil

1 cinnamon stick

1 stalk lemongrass, center white part only, cut into 2-inch (5-cm) pieces

2–2½ lb (1–1.25 kg) beef chuck roast, cut into 1-inch (2.5-cm) cubes

1 can (13½ fl oz/425 ml) unsweetened coconut milk

1 tablespoon soy sauce

1 tablespoon sugar

1 teaspoon salt

The sauce for this stew is dry, meaning that it coats the meat at the end of cooking. The recipe calls for ten to fifteen dried red chiles. Ten is a nice wake-up call; fifteen will clear your sinuses. Tangy Mango Relish (page 58) or diced fresh pineapple is a refreshing match for this incendiary stew. Accompany it as well with steamed rice to help temper the heat.

SERVES 6

❈ Place the chiles in a small bowl, add warm water to cover, and let stand until soft, 10 minutes. Drain. Place the candlenuts or almonds in a small bowl, add warm water to cover, and let stand until moist, about 5 minutes. Drain.

❈ In a blender, combine the chiles, candlenuts or almonds, shallots, garlic, galangal, chopped lemongrass, ginger, shrimp or anchovy paste, coriander, cumin, turmeric, fennel, and cloves. Add 2 tablespoons water or just enough to facilitate blending. Process until a smooth paste forms.

❈ In a small, dry frying pan over medium heat, toast the coconut, stirring constantly, until golden brown, 3–5 minutes. Let cool.

❈ In a dutch oven over medium-high heat, warm the oil. Add the spice paste and cook, stirring constantly, until the paste is aromatic and beads of oil separate from the paste, 3–5 minutes. Add the cinnamon stick, toasted coconut, and lemongrass pieces, and cook, stirring occasionally, for 1 minute. Add the beef and toss and stir to coat the cubes evenly, about 5 minutes. Add the coconut milk, soy sauce, sugar, and salt and bring to a boil, stirring constantly. Reduce the heat to low and simmer, uncovered, stirring occasionally, until the meat is tender, 1–1½ hours. If the sauce begins to dry out before the meat is done, add a little hot water.

❈ Raise the heat to medium-high and cook until the sauce is thick and oily, 5–10 minutes. Fry the meat in the sauce until lightly browned, about 5 minutes. The sauce should coat the meat.

❈ Divide among individual bowls and serve.

NUTRITIONAL ANALYSIS PER SERVING: Calories 675 (Kilojoules 2,835); Protein 32 g; Carbohydrates 12 g; Total Fat 56 g; Saturated Fat 29 g; Cholesterol 123 mg; Sodium 736 mg; Dietary Fiber 1 g

Miso-Glazed Sea Bass

PREP TIME: 15 MINUTES, PLUS
2 HOURS FOR MARINATING

COOKING TIME: 10 MINUTES

INGREDIENTS

½ cup (4 oz/125 g) white miso

¼ cup (2 fl oz/60 ml) mirin

¼ cup (2 fl oz/60 ml) sake

3 tablespoons sugar

1 teaspoon peeled and finely grated
fresh ginger

6 Chilean sea bass fillets, about 6 oz
(185 g) each, ¾–1 inch (2–2.5 cm)
thick

1 teaspoon finely grated lemon zest

COOKING TIP: This recipe also works
very well with other firm-fleshed
white fish fillets such as halibut,
swordfish, or cod. It is also excellent
with richer tasting fish, particularly
salmon and tuna.

The fermented soybean paste called miso, a staple of Japanese cooking, is used in salad dressings; as a pickling agent; as a base for soups; and, as here, to flavor marinades. Combined with mirin and sake—Japanese wines made from rice—and flecked with fresh ginger, the marinade is brushed on the fish during cooking to create a shimmering, subtly sweet, and rich savory glaze.

SERVES 6

❁ In a shallow glass baking dish, whisk together the miso, mirin, sake, sugar, and ginger until smooth. Add the sea bass and turn to coat evenly. Cover and refrigerate for at least 2 hours or up to overnight.

❁ Preheat a broiler (griller).

❁ Remove the sea bass from the marinade, reserving the marinade. Place the fillets on a broiler pan and broil (grill) 2–3 inches (5–7.5 cm) from the heat source until browned with crusty edges, about 4 minutes. Turn, brush with the reserved marinade, and grill until browned on the second side, 3–4 minutes.

❁ Sprinkle with the lemon zest and serve.

NUTRITIONAL ANALYSIS PER SERVING: Calories 268 (Kilojoules 1,201); Protein 34 g; Carbohydrates 16 g; Total Fat 5 g; Saturated Fat 1 g; Cholesterol 70 mg; Sodium 806 mg; Dietary Fiber 1 g

Mango and Pineapple Sorbet

PREP TIME: 10 MINUTES, PLUS
1½ HOURS FOR FREEZING

INGREDIENTS

2 mangoes, peeled and pitted, plus thin slices for garnish

⅔ cup (5 oz/155 g) sugar

3 tablespoons lime juice

1 cup (6 oz/185 g) finely chopped fresh pineapple

PREP TIP: If you do not have an ice-cream maker, pour the purée into a 9-by-12-inch (23-by-30-cm) metal cake pan (or two 8-inch/20-cm square pans). Freeze until almost solid, 1–1½ hours. Using a plastic spatula or large spoon, break up and process in a food processor, pulsing until smooth, light, and fluffy; do not overbeat. Pour into an airtight container and freeze.

No pairing of fruits is more Southeast Asian than mango and pineapple. In this Western-influenced recipe, the fruits are accented with lime and made into a sorbet. Ices are not as foreign to Asia as you might think. According to history, the ancient Chinese made flavored ices long before the Italians perfected the popular dessert.

SERVES 8

✤ In a blender or food processor, purée the 2 mangoes. You should have about 3 cups (24 oz/750 g). Add the sugar and lime juice and process to combine. Transfer to a large bowl and stir in the pineapple.

✤ Pour the mixture into an ice-cream maker and freeze according to the manufacturer's directions until firm, about 30 minutes. Transfer to an airtight container and freeze until ready to serve.

✤ To serve, scoop the sorbet into chilled bowls and garnish with the mango slices.

NUTRITIONAL ANALYSIS PER SERVING: Calories 114 (Kilojoules 479); Protein 0 g; Carbohydrates 30 g; Total Fat 0 g; Saturated Fat 0 g; Cholesterol 0 mg; Sodium 2 mg; Dietary Fiber 1 g

Coconut-Banana Pancake Rolls

PREP TIME: 45 MINUTES

COOKING TIME: 20 MINUTES

INGREDIENTS

FOR THE PANCAKES

1 cup (5 oz/155 g) all-purpose
   (plain) flour

¼ cup (2 oz/60 g) granulated sugar

2 tablespoons unsweetened
   shredded dried coconut

1 teaspoon baking powder

¼ teaspoon salt

1 small ripe banana, mashed

1 egg, lightly beaten

1¾–2 cups (14–16 fl oz/430–500 ml)
   unsweetened thin coconut milk

3 tablespoons vegetable oil, or more
   if needed

FOR THE FILLING

¼ cup (2 oz/60 g) unsalted butter

3 large bananas, halved lengthwise,
   then each half cut crosswise in half

6 tablespoons (2½ oz/75 g) lightly
   packed brown sugar

6 tablespoons (3 fl oz/90 ml) lime
   juice

2 tablespoons toasted unsweetened
   shaved or shredded dried coconut

For this tempting Thai-inspired dessert, pancakes made with banana and coconut milk are wrapped around fried bananas and served hot.

SERVES 6

✽ To make the pancakes, in a large bowl, combine the flour, granulated sugar, coconut, baking powder, and salt. Add the mashed banana, egg, and 1¾ cups (14 fl oz/430 ml) of the coconut milk and stir to combine. The batter should have a thin consistency. If it is too thick, add some or all of the remaining ¼ cup (2 fl oz/70 ml) coconut milk.

✽ Preheat an oven to 200°F (95°C).

✽ Heat a large frying pan over medium heat until a few drops of water sprinkled on the pan immediately form beads that dance across the surface. Add 1 or 2 teaspoons oil, tilt the pan to coat the bottom, and wipe off the excess with several layers of paper towels. Filling a ¼-cup (2–fl oz/60-ml) measuring cup for each pancake, pour the batter in the pan. Leave space between the pancakes and cook until large bubbles appear on the tops and the bottoms are lightly browned, about 1½ minutes. Turn and cook until browned on the second side, about 1 minute longer. Transfer to a plate, cover loosely with aluminum foil, and keep warm in the oven. Cook the remaining pancakes, using additional oil if necessary. You should have 12 pancakes.

✽ To make the filling, in a frying pan over medium-high heat, melt the butter. When the butter is almost sizzling, add the halved bananas and cook, stirring occasionally, until lightly browned, about 1 minute. Sprinkle the brown sugar over the bananas and gently shake the pan until the sugar is dissolved. Stir in the lime juice.

✽ Place 1 banana piece on each pancake and roll the pancake around the banana. Arrange 2 rolls on each plate, spoon some of the pan juices on top, sprinkle with the toasted coconut, and serve hot.

NUTRITIONAL ANALYSIS PER SERVING: Calories 532 (Kilojoules 2,234); Protein 6 g; Carbohydrates 62 g; Total Fat 32 g; Saturated Fat 24 g; Cholesterol 72 mg; Sodium 265 mg; Dietary Fiber 2 g

Black Sticky Rice with Coconut Cream

PREP TIME: 15 MINUTES, PLUS
4 HOURS FOR SOAKING

COOKING TIME: 1 HOUR

INGREDIENTS

2 cups (14 oz/440 g) black sticky rice

2¼ cups (18 fl oz/560 ml) cold water

1 can (13½ fl oz/425 ml) unsweetened coconut milk, well shaken

⅔ cup (5 oz/155 g) granulated sugar

½ teaspoon salt

½ cup (3½ oz/105 g) palm sugar or
brown sugar

½ cup (2 oz/60 g) toasted unsweetened shaved or shredded coconut
or ½ cup (3 oz/90 g) chopped
roasted peanuts, for garnish

8 sprigs fresh mint leaves, for
garnish

Thai sticky, or glutinous, rice is available in white or black grains. The latter type, used predominantly for desserts, has a particularly nutty flavor and texture. When cooked, black sticky rice turns a magnificent aubergine in color. If you cannot find black sticky rice, use white sticky rice for this simple but luscious dessert. The results will still be excellent.

SERVES 8

✺ Pick over the rice and discard any stones or impurities. Rinse thoroughly and drain. Combine the rice and the cold water in a 2½-qt (2.5-l) saucepan and let stand for at least 4 hours or as long as overnight.

✺ Bring the rice and its soaking water to a boil over high heat, stirring to loosen the grains from the pan bottom. Continue cooking over high heat until all the surface water is absorbed, 3–5 minutes. Cover, reduce the heat to low, and cook until the grains are chewy to the bite, 35–45 minutes, depending on how long the rice was soaked in water. Remove from the heat and let stand, without stirring, for at least 10 minutes.

✺ In a saucepan over high heat, combine half of the coconut milk, the granulated sugar, and the salt. Bring to a boil, stirring frequently, then pour into a large mixing bowl. Add two-thirds of the cooked rice and stir gently to combine. Continue adding rice just until there is no longer enough coconut milk to coat the grains.

✺ In a small saucepan over high heat, combine the remaining coconut milk and the palm or brown sugar and cook, stirring frequently, until reduced to a thick cream, about 5 minutes.

✺ Divide the rice among 8 bowls. Spoon the thick cream over the rice and sprinkle with the coconut or peanuts. Garnish with mint sprigs and serve.

NUTRITIONAL ANALYSIS PER SERVING: Calories 443 (Kilojoules 1,861); Protein 5 g; Carbohydrates 74 g; Total Fat 15 g; Saturated Fat 13 g; Cholesterol 0 mg; Sodium 159 mg; Dietary Fiber 2 g

Orange Slices in Rose Flower Water

PREP TIME: 20 MINUTES, PLUS
1 HOUR FOR CHILLING

INGREDIENTS

6 navel oranges

2 tablespoons honey

juice of 1 large lime

1½ teaspoons sugar

1 teaspoon rose flower water

pesticide-free rose petals or mint
leaves, for garnish

In China, oranges are esteemed for their round shape and gold color. Symbols of good fortune, orange wedges are served as the finale to humble and grand meals alike. In this dessert, they are given just a bit more flair with a light syrup accented with rose flower water, a popular flavoring in India and Thailand.

SERVES 6

❀ Using a small, sharp knife, cut a slice off the top and bottom of each orange to expose the fruit. Place upright on a cutting board and slice off the peel in strips to expose the flesh. Cut each orange crosswise into thin slices and put into a bowl. Using a large spoon, hold the orange slices and pour the juices into a small bowl.

❀ Whisk the honey into the orange juice. Add the lime juice, sugar, and rose flower water to the honey mixture and whisk thoroughly. Pour over the orange slices, cover, and refrigerate for at least 1 hour or up to overnight.

❀ To serve, divide among dessert plates, spooning the syrup over the slices. Garnish with rose petals or mint leaves.

NUTRITIONAL ANALYSIS PER SERVING: Calories 92 (Kilojoules 386); Protein 1 g; Carbohydrates 24 g; Total Fat 0 g; Saturated Fat 0 g; Cholesterol 0 mg; Sodium 2 mg; Dietary Fiber 3 g

Honeydew-Tapioca Soup

PREP TIME: 20 MINUTES, PLUS
30 MINUTES FOR SOAKING
AND 3 HOURS FOR CHILLING

COOKING TIME: 15 MINUTES

INGREDIENTS

½ cup (2 oz/60 g) small tapioca pearls

4 cups (32 fl oz/1 l) water

¾ cup (6 oz/185 g) sugar

large pinch of salt

2 cups (16 fl oz/500 ml) unsweetened coconut milk

1 very ripe honeydew melon

Wait for the height of the melon season when honeydew is very sweet to make this refreshing cold fruit soup, a popular dish in Asia. Use the uniformly round tapioca pearls sold in Asian markets rather than the quick-cooking variety commonly found in food stores.

SERVES 8

✺ In a small bowl, combine the tapioca and 2 cups (16 fl oz/500 ml) of the water and let stand for about 30 minutes. Drain and rinse. In a saucepan over high heat, combine the tapioca, remaining 2 cups (16 fl oz/500 ml) water, sugar, and salt and bring to a boil, stirring constantly. Reduce the heat to low and simmer, stirring often, until the tapioca pearls are transparent, 10–12 minutes. Stir in the coconut milk and let stand until cool. Cover and refrigerate for at least 3 hours or up to 3 days.

✺ Using a small melon baller, cut one-third of the melon into small balls. Alternatively, cut into ¼-inch (6-mm) cubes. In a food processor or blender, purée the remaining melon flesh. Stir the melon purée and balls or cubes into the chilled tapioca. Keep refrigerated until ready to serve.

✺ Spoon into individual bowls and serve thoroughly chilled.

NUTRITIONAL ANALYSIS PER SERVING: Calories 276 (Kilojoules 1,159); Protein 2 g; Carbohydrates 44 g; Total Fat 12 g; Saturated Fat 11 g; Cholesterol 0 mg; Sodium 85 mg; Dietary Fiber 1 g

GLOSSARY

BANANA LEAVES

Southeast Asian cooks use the large leaves of the banana plant as wrappers in which foods may be steamed, boiled, or roasted, gaining, in the process, a delicate, sweet flavor and sometimes a green tint. The leaves also make attractive liners for serving platters. Fresh leaves are occasionally sold in Asian markets; more often, they are available frozen in packages, to be defrosted at room temperature as needed. Wipe both fresh and defrosted leaves thoroughly with a clean, damp cloth. Fresh green corn husks, or dried corn husks soaked in cold water until pliable, may be substituted.

BASIL, THAI

The dark green leaves and purple-tinged stems of this variety of fresh basil are more aromatic than the variety known as sweet basil, which may be

substituted. The leaves are added to hot, savory dishes just before serving for a burst of flavor and scent.

BONITO FLAKES, DRIED

Known in Japanese as *katsuobushi*, these almost transparent shavings are cut from blocks of dried bonito fish. Valued as a flavoring for broths and sauces and as a garnish, the flakes have a heady taste and scent somewhat reminiscent of smoked bacon. The shavings are sold already cut and packaged in cellophane; look for those with a pale color and good aroma. Once opened, they will keep in the refrigerator for several weeks. For even better flavor, look for whole blocks of dried bonito, which must be cut with a special shaving tool sold in Asian markets that carry the blocks.

CANDLENUTS

Resembling small, peeled hazelnuts, these waxy, oily nuts—known in Malaysia as *buah keras* and in Indonesia as *kemiri*—are often ground and used to thicken spice pastes. The name derives from use of the nuts to make

candles, a practice still followed in some areas. If you cannot find candlenuts in Indian or Indonesian markets, substitute blanched almonds or unsalted macadamia or Brazil nuts.

CHICKPEA FLOUR

Also known as garbanzo flour, this ground form of dried chickpeas (garbanzo beans) is used as a thickener for some curry sauces. You'll find it most readily in well-stocked Italian delicatessens, as well as in Indian markets (labeled *channa dal flour*) and in Middle Eastern stores (labeled *besan*).

CHILI OIL

Made by infusing dried, hot red chile peppers in vegetable oil or sesame oil, this fragrant, spicy seasoning is used to flavor a wide range of savory dishes. It is sold in Asian markets and well-stocked food stores.

EQUIPMENT

MORTAR AND PESTLE
Consisting of a durable, heavy bowl (the mortar)—made of marble or another stone or ceramic—and a cylindrical hand-held pounder (the pestle) of similar material, this ancient kitchen implement still provides an ideal way to grind ingredients into fine powders or pastes. This Japanese mortar and pestle is used for dry ingredients only.

STEAMER BASKET, BAMBOO
A cylindrical, flat-bottomed basket made from loosely woven strips of bamboo held in a stiff bamboo frame, this Asian utensil is used to steam a variety of foods ranging in size from small dumplings to whole fish. Small steamer baskets are made to fit atop a saucepan of simmering water; larger ones can be set inside a wok.

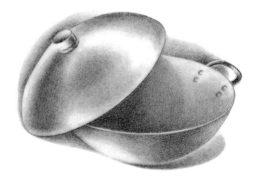

WOK
A Chinese cooking vessel used for stir-frying, this hemispherical pan is traditionally made of heavy milled steel to hold heat well and conduct it evenly. Modern woks are made of stainless steel or aluminum and have nonstick surfaces. A domed lid is used on the wok when food must be covered while cooking.

COCONUT CREAM AND MILK

Coconut milk, extracted from the freshly grated, snow-white flesh of the coconut, is used to add rich, slightly sweet flavor to a wide variety of Southeast Asian dishes, both savory and sweet. Look in Asian markets for cans or bottles of unsweetened coconut milk.

Coconut cream is the thick, rich layer of fat that rises to the top of a container of coconut milk. It may be spooned off to use on its own when extra richness is required for a recipe or discarded when somewhat lighter coconut milk is desired. For most recipes, containers of coconut milk should be shaken before opening to blend the cream into the milk. Opened coconut milk will keep in the refrigerator for 2 days.

CURRY PASTE, THAI

Sold in cans or jars in Asian markets, these ready-to-use, oil-based Thai spice blends combine green or red chile peppers with other seasonings such as garlic, onions, lemongrass, cilantro, and galangal.

DAIKON

Prized for its refreshing sweet-hot bite and as an aid to digestion, this long white Japanese radish is grated and used raw as a garnish for noodle dishes, or in tempura dipping broth, and is sliced and cooked in broths and stews. Large, whole fresh daikon roots are sold in Asian markets, farmers' markets, and well-stocked food stores. *(See photo, page 10.)*

FISH SAUCE

Used in Southeast Asian kitchens much as Chinese and Japanese cooks use soy sauce, fish sauce is a thin, amber-colored liquid made from salted and fermented fish. Although it varies slightly from country to country, all fish sauces are interchangeable. The most commonly available varieties are Thai fish sauce (*nam pla*) and Vietnamese fish sauce (*nuoc mam*).

FIVE-SPICE POWDER

Sold in well-stocked food stores and Asian markets, this commercial blend of spices is a popular seasoning in Chinese kitchens. The most common five ingredients are star anise, Sichuan peppercorns, cloves, cinnamon, and fennel seeds.

GALANGAL

A relative of ginger, this brown, knobbly rhizome has a slightly medicinal, mustardlike flavor and is used in simmered Thai and other Southeast Asian dishes. It is sold in Asian markets in both fresh and sliced, dried forms; when using dried galangal, halve the quantity called for in a recipe and soak the slices in warm water until pliable. Galangal is also known as Siamese ginger, *kha* in Thailand, and *lengkuas* in Indonesia and Malaysia. *(See photo, page 10.)*

GHEE

Prized as a cooking fat in India for its rich, nutlike flavor, this form of clarified butter is slowly simmered to eliminate moisture, a process that browns it slightly. Containers of ghee are sold in Indian markets.

GINGER

This spicy-sweet rhizome, mistakenly referred to as a root, is widely used in Asian cuisines. When using **fresh ginger**, peel off the papery brown skin before slicing or grating. Thin slices of **pickled ginger**, which have a light pink color, are used by Japanese cooks as a garnish. They are widely sold in well-stocked food stores and Japanese markets.

KAFFIR LIME LEAVES

The leaves of a small, spherical, gnarled-looking variety of lime native to Southeast Asia contribute a powerful citrus aroma and flavor to curries and other simmered dishes. The leaves are used fresh, frozen, or dried. If necessary, substitute the clean, pesticide-free leaves of other citrus varieties. You can also use 1½ teaspoons finely grated lime zest for every 2 leaves called for in a recipe. *(See photo, page 10.)*

LEMONGRASS

The stiff, reedlike stalks of this Southeast Asian plant, now also cultivated in the West, impart a citrusy perfume to simmered and stir-fried dishes. You can find fresh lemongrass in Asian markets and well-stocked food stores. If a recipe calls for the heart of lemongrass, use only the bottom 4–6 inches (10–15 cm) of the stalk and peel off the tough outer leaves until you reach an inner purple ring. Crushing the stalk or chopping it will help release its aromatic oils.

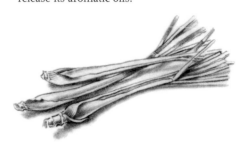

LILY BUDS, DRIED

These dried flower buds of a variety of daylily, also known as tiger lily buds and golden needles, contribute a subtle, slightly sharp and sour taste and a chewy texture to Chinese soups and other dishes. They may be found packaged in cellophane bags in Chinese food stores.

MINT, VIETNAMESE

This highly aromatic herb is added fresh to Vietnamese-style salads, spring rolls, and other dishes. A combination of spearmint and fresh cilantro (fresh coriander) may be substituted.

MIRIN

Extracted from fermented sweet rice and usually referred to as sweet rice wine, amber-colored mirin is a popular seasoning in Japanese kitchens. Store bottles of mirin away from heat and light to safeguard their flavor and color.

MUSHROOMS

Asian cooks use a wide variety of fresh and dried mushrooms, including those called for in this book, all available in Asian markets and well-stocked food stores.

CHINESE BLACK, DRIED

Hearty in flavor and texture, this is the dried form of the now-popular mushroom known by the Japanese name shiitake. The dried mushrooms, actually dark brown in color, are reconstituted in warm water until tender, after which their tough stems are trimmed away.

ENOKI, FRESH

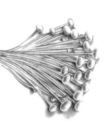

These tiny, slender, pale ivory mushrooms are a popular garnish in Japanese kitchens.

SHIITAKE, FRESH AND DRIED

Now widely cultivated, these dark brown, meaty mushrooms are found fresh in most markets. The dried

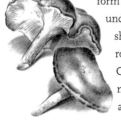

form is packaged under the name of shiitake mushrooms and as Chinese black mushrooms (see above).

TREE EAR, DRIED

Also known as wood ear and black fungus—and in a larger form as cloud ear—these delicately flavored dried mushrooms have a somewhat earlike shape and a crinkly texture resembling the bark of a tree. Those with the finest taste are usually the smaller specimens with a uniform black color. Reconstitute them in warm water until pliable and trim off their tough portions before use.

NOODLES

Made from several different flours and other ingredients, and cut in a wide variety of shapes, noodles are popular ingredients in all Asian kitchens. Look for them in Asian markets and well-stocked food stores.

Bean thread vermicelli, sometimes labeled simply as "bean threads," are very thin, transparent noodles made from vegetable starch such as that of mung beans (for Chinese *fen si* or *sai fun*) or potatoes and corn (for Japanese *harusame*). The dried noodles become silken and tender when cooked in liquid or crisp and puffy when deep-fried. Also known as cellophane, glass, mirror, or transparent noodles. *(See photo, page 10.)* Typified by the Japanese soba, **buckwheat** noodles are usually sold dried but may also sometimes be found fresh. Made of brown buckwheat flour mixed with a little wheat flour and occasionally such flavorings as green tea or sweet Japanese mountain yam, they have a robust, earthy taste with a slightly sour tang. *(See photo, page 11.)* **Chinese-style egg** noodles, known by the Chinese name *dan mein*, are thick noodles made fresh from a dough of wheat flour and eggs. *(See photo, page 11.)* A Malaysian variety of thick, round, fresh Chinese-style noodles, **Hokkien** is made from wheat flour, eggs, and water. **Mung bean** is another common way of referring to Chinese bean thread vermicelli (see above). Dried flat noodle ribbons or thin wiry threads known as **rice ribbon**, **stick**, or **vermicelli**, are made from a flour ground from rice that has been cooked and then dried. Before use, they require soaking in cold water until pliable. *(See photos, pages 10–11.)* **Shanghai-style**, a variety of fresh Chinese noodles made from a wheat-flour dough formed into thick strands and characterized by their chewy texture. *(See photo, page 10.)*

OYSTER SAUCE

Oysters are cooked with soy sauce and salt to make this thick, flavorful seasoning from the Chinese city of Canton. It is a popular ingredient in stir-fry sauces.

PALM SUGAR

Sold in the form of tubs, cakes, or lumps, this coarse, sticky, deep amber sugar is made by boiling the sap of various types of palm trees, particularly the palmyra palm. Sold in Asian markets, it is also known as jaggery or coconut sugar. If unavailable, substitute dark brown sugar.

RED BEAN CURD

Also known as fermented bean curd or tofu, this commercial Chinese product is made by fermenting cubes of bean curd with a specific type of mold, which gives the cubes a rich, almost cheeselike aroma and texture. The bean curd is sold in bottles, afloat in a brine sometimes seasoned with flakes of hot red chili. Store in the refrigerator after opening.

RICE PAPER ROUNDS

Usually made from a dough of rice flour and water, these paper-thin, brittle, translucent edible wrappers are soaked in cold water until soft before use. Rice papers are sold in large rounds that vary in diameter from 6½ to 14 inches (16.5 to 35 cm).

RICE, STICKY

This short-grain variety of rice is rich in surface starch that produces a sticky consistency when cooked. Polished white and black-husked forms are available in Asian markets and are particularly favored by Thai cooks for savory and sweet dishes.

RICE VINEGAR

Made from rice wine, this clear vinegar is enjoyed throughout Asia for the fresh, clean, light taste it gives to sauces, dressings, and pickles. Available unseasoned and seasoned with sugar and salt, rice vinegar is produced primarily in Japan, where it tends to be mild in taste, and also in China, which produces somewhat stronger products.

RICE WINE

Chinese wine made from fermented rice is noted for its deep amber color, rich aroma, and sweet, nutty flavor. It is aged about ten years and can be drunk, like **sake**, or used in cooking. Dry sherry is an acceptable substitute. Mirin *(page 109)*, a Japanese rice wine, has a milder, more syrupy flavor.

ROSE FLOWER WATER

Extracted from rose petals, this sweet essence is used as a flavoring for desserts and confections in the Indian subcontinent.

SAKE

Made from fermented rice, this Japanese dry wine is enjoyed warm or cold and unfiltered with meals, and is used as an ingredient in marinades and sauces. You can find sake in Asian markets as well as in well-stocked liquor and wine shops.

SESAME OIL, ASIAN

Sold in small bottles in Asian markets and well-stocked food stores, this oil is pressed from sesame seeds. Oil made from toasted seeds is a dark amber color with a full, rich, nutty flavor. It is used almost always as a seasoning. Do not substitute sesame oil made from untoasted seeds.

SHRIMP PASTES

Shrimp (prawns) are salted, sun-dried, and fermented to make this pungent Southeast Asian seasoning, which ranges in color from light brown to purplish black. Thai- and Chinese-style shrimp pastes are generally softer and are sold packed in small tubs. Malaysian shrimp paste, known as blachan, is sold in the form of compact, hard bricks. Anchovy paste may be substituted if shrimp paste is unavailable.

SHRIMP, PEELING AND DEVEINING

Before cooking, fresh shrimp (prawns) are usually peeled of their brittle shells and deveined. To peel a shrimp, split open the shell by pulling it apart with your thumbs along the concave underside, between the rows of legs. To devein a shrimp, use the tip of a small, sharp knife to slit the shrimp along its convex back, exposing the pale gray to black, veinlike intestinal tract; with your fingertips or the knife, pull out and discard the vein.

SOY SAUCES

Many different Asian cuisines employ as a seasoning this dark-colored liquid made by fermenting and aging soybeans, roasted wheat or barley, salt, and water. Chinese cooks use products known as dark or medium soy sauce, which includes a little caramel to give it a sweeter flavor, thicker texture, and darker color; and light, thin, or regular soy sauce, which has a more fluid consistency and mild taste. Soy sauces from Japan tend to have milder, sweeter, less salty flavors than Chinese products.

SRIRACHA SAUCE

Named for the Thai coastal town of Sri Racha, this popular commercial chili sauce resembles an orange-red ketchup and is a powerful source of garlic-spiked heat in the kitchen and on the dining table. It is sold in Asian markets in large plastic squeeze bottles.

STAR ANISE

The seedpods of a tree related to the magnolia, this popular Asian spice has a sweet, highly aromatic flavor somewhat akin to that of the aniseed. A whole pod of star anise is composed of eight points, each of which contains a seed. Sold in jars or cellophane packets, the pods may be added whole to simmered dishes, or individual points may be broken off. Asian markets also sell jars of ground star anise.

SUGARCANE

Fresh sticks of sugarcane, sold in the produce departments of Asian markets and well-stocked food stores, are popularly used in Southeast Asia as skewers for grilled foods, imparting a subtly sweet flavor. Canned sticks are also available. *(See photo, page 10.)*

TAMARIND PULP

Mild and sweet-tart in flavor. Water made from the pulp is used in cooking. To make tamarind water, cover a 1-inch (2.5-cm) chunk of tamarind pulp with ⅓ cup (3 fl oz/80 ml) hot water. With a fork, break up the pulp and let it steep for 5 minutes. Pour the mixture into a fine-mesh strainer placed over a container and press to extract the water into the container. Discard the pulp.

TOFU

Enjoyed throughout Asia as a protein-rich stand-in for meat, tofu, also known as bean curd, is made by adding a coagulating agent to a milky mixture of ground soybeans and water. The resulting solids are formed into rectangular or cube-shaped cakes characterized by their very mild flavor and soft, creamy texture. Chinese bean curd tends to have a firmer consistency than the Japanese variety.

WASABI POWDER

Ground to a fine powder from a dried variety of powerful green horseradish, this Japanese seasoning is usually reconstituted with a little water to form a smooth paste that is used to flavor sushi and dipping sauces.

WATER CHESTNUTS

These small, roughly spherical tubers are prized in Chinese and other Asian kitchens for their refreshingly crisp texture and mildly earthy, sweet flavor. Look in Asian markets for fresh water chestnuts, which require careful peeling of their dark brown skins before use; they have a far more pleasing taste and texture than their canned, peeled counterparts.

INDEX

ACKNOWLEDGMENTS

The publishers would like to thank the following people and associations for their generous assistance and support in producing this book:
Desne Border, Linda Bouchard, Ken DellaPenta, and Hill Nutrition Associates.

The following kindly lent props for photography: Fillamento, Williams-Sonoma, and The Gardener. The photographer would like to thank
Sarah Hammond for generously sharing her lovely home in Bolinas, CA, for location photography. He would also like to thank Chromeworks
and ProCamera, San Francisco, CA, and FUJI Film for their generous support of this project.